KRYSIA

KRYSIA

A Polish Girl's Stolen Childhood During World War II

KRYSTYNA MIHULKA
with Krystyna Poray Goddu

Published by Chicago Review Press Incorporated
814 North Franklin Street
Chicago, Illinois 60610
ISBN 978-1-61373-441-4

Library of Congress Cataloging-in-Publication Data
Names: Mihulka, Krystyna, 1930- author. | Goddu, Krystyna Poray, co-author.
Title: Krysia : a Polish girl's stolen childhood during World War II / Krystyna Mihulka with Krystyna Poray Goddu.
Description: Chicago, Illinois : Chicago Review Press, 2017. | Audience: Ages 10 to 13.
Identifiers: LCCN 2016016685 (print) | LCCN 2016023843 (ebook) | ISBN 9781613734414 (cloth : alkaline paper) | ISBN 9781613734421 (pdf) | ISBN 9781613734445 (epub) | ISBN 9781613734438 (kindle)
Subjects: LCSH: Mihulka, Krystyna, 1930—Childhood and youth—Juvenile literature. | Mihulka, Krystyna, 1930—Family—Juvenile literature. | World War, 1939-1945—Personal narratives, Polish—Juvenile literature. | Girls—Poland—Lwów—Biography—Juvenile literature. | Lwów (Poland)—Biography—Juvenile literature. | World War, 1914-1918—Deportations from Poland—Juvenile literature. | World War, 1939-1945—Prisoners and prisons, Soviet—Juvenile literature. | Collective farms—Kazakhstan—History—20th century—Juvenile literature. | Forced labor—Kazakhstan—History—20th century—Juvenile literature. | World War, 1939-1945—Refugees—Juvenile literature. | BISAC: JUVENILE NONFICTION / Biography & Autobiography / Women. | JUVENILE NONFICTION /
Biography & Autobiography / Historical. | JUVENILE NONFICTION / History / Europe.
Classification: LCC D811.5 .M442 2017 (print) | LCC D811.5 (ebook) | DDC 940.53/4779 [B] —dc23
LC record available at https://lccn.loc.gov/2016016685

Interior design: Sarah Olson
Interior map: Chris Erichsen

Printed in the United States of America
5 4 3 2 1

In memory of my mother, Zofia Mihulka (1902–1995),
and my father, Andrzej Mihulka (1899–1944)
—K.M.

In memory of Janina Balicka (1924–1942) and
Zofia M. Biernacki-Poray (1923–2016)
—K.P.G.

Contents

PART III: LIFE IN CAPTIVITY

PART IV: FLIGHT TO FREEDOM

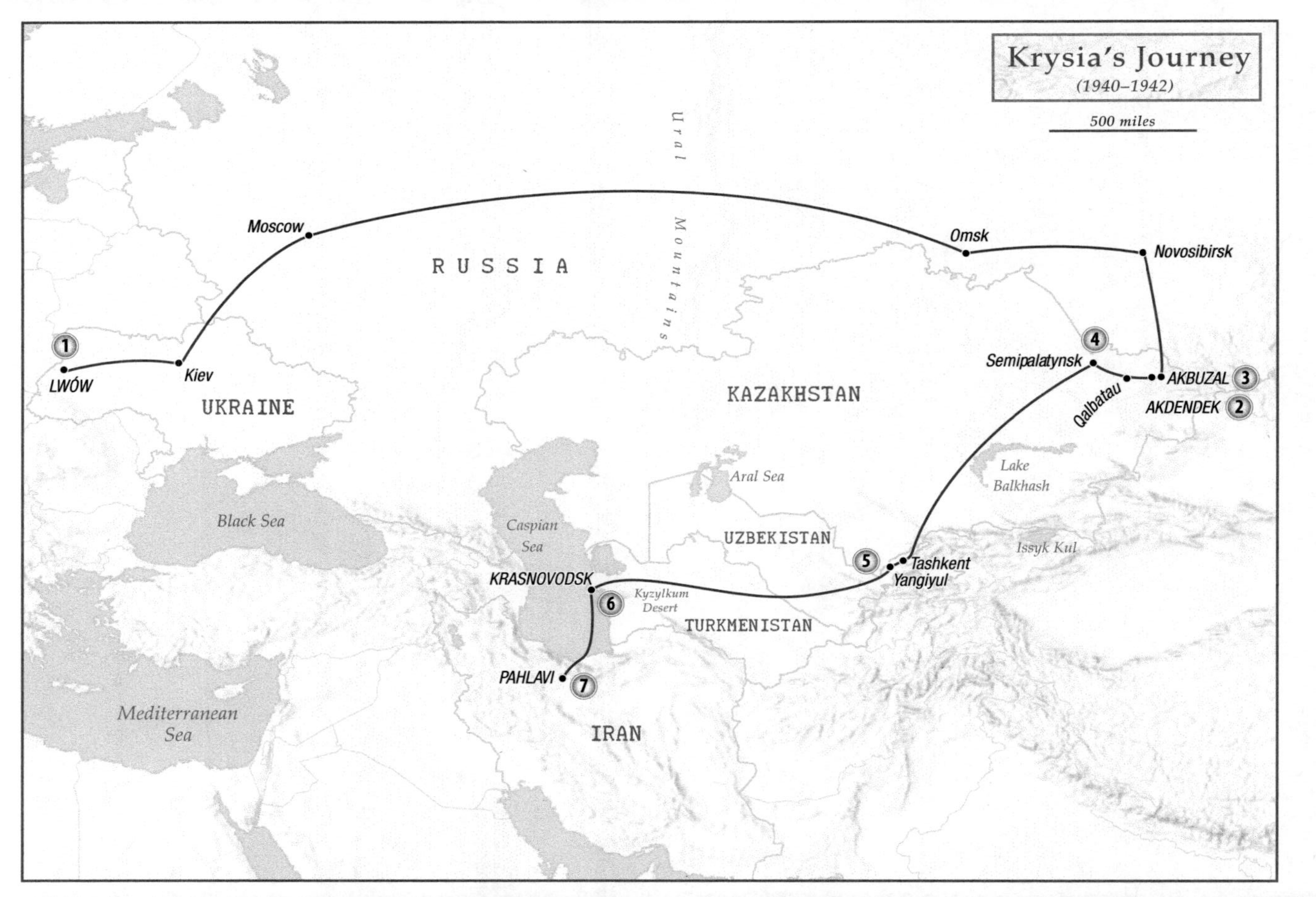

Krysia's Journey
(1940–1942)
500 miles
Ural Mountains
RUSSIA
UKRAINE
KAZAKHSTAN
UZBEKISTAN
TURKMENISTAN
IRAN
1 LWÓW
Kiev
Moscow
Omsk
Novosibirsk
3 AKBUZAL
2 AKDENDEK
Qalbatau
4 Semipalatynsk
Lake Balkhash
Issyk Kul
Aral Sea
5 Tashkent
Yangiyul
6 KRASNOVODSK
Kyzylkum Desert
Caspian Sea
7 PAHLAVI
Black Sea
Mediterranean Sea

A Polish Pronunciation and Vocabulary Guide

The Polish language has different pronunciation rules from those of the English language. For example, *w* is pronounced "v" and the *si* and *sz* combinations are both pronounced "sh," while *cz* is pronounced "ch." In Polish the *c* in *ch* is silent. The letter *c* is always soft, like in *celery*. The letter *y* is pronounced like a short *i*, as in *kitten*, while the letter *i* is pronounced like a long *e*, as in *tree*. Below is a guide to pronouncing the Polish words and names that appear in this book, and definitions for the Polish words and phrases. Another point to note is that when Polish people address each other, the ending of the name changes to *u*. You will notice in the book that when I speak to my mother or father, I call them "Mamusiu" or "Tatusiu" and they call me "Krysiu."

Babcia (Bab-cha)—Grandmother

Boże, zlituj się (Bo-zhe, zlee-tuy-shewn)—God, have mercy

Cicha noc (Chee-ha noc)—Silent night

Ciocia (Cho-cha)—Aunt

Danusia (Da-noo-sha)

Do widzenia (Do veed-zenya)—Good-bye (see you soon)

Dobrze (Dob-zhe)—Okay

Drochobycz (Dro-ho-bich)

Dziękuję bardzo (Dzhen-koo-ye bardzho)—Thank you very much

Dzień dobry (Dzhen do-bry)—Good day, or good morning

Ewa (Eva)

Graźyna (Gra-zhi-na)

Janek (Yah-nek)

Jędruś (Yen-droosh)

Jeszcze Polska nie zginęła pòki my źyjemy (Yesh-che Pol-ska nee-eh zgee-ne-la pu-kee my zhi-ye-my)—Poland is not lost so long as we still live

Krysia (Kri-sha, like Tricia with a *k*)

Lećmy do domu (Lech my do domu)—Let's rush home

Ludwik (Lood-veek)

Lusia (Loo-sha)

Lwów (Lvoov)

Mamusia (Ma-moo-sha)—Mommy

Marysia (Ma-ri-sha)
Mila (Mee-la)
Na zdrowie (Na zdrov-ye)—To your/our health
Nie (Nee-eh)—No
Nie bójcie się (Nee-eh boy-che shewn)—Don't be afraid
Opłatek (O-pla-tik)—Blessed wafer
Pan (Pan)—Mr. (polite form of addressing an adult man)
Pani (Panee)—Miss or Mrs. (polite form of addressing an adult woman)
Pomoc (Po-moc)—Help
Proszę wychodzić (Pro-she vy-hodzh-eech)—Please come out
Starucha (Sta-ru-ha)—Old lady
Szybko (Shib-ko)—Hurry
Tak (Tahk)—Yes
Tatuś (Ta-toosh)—Daddy
Tocha (To-ha)
Wedel (Ve-del)
Wesołych Swiąt (Ve-so-wyh Shvee-ont)—Happy Holidays (said only at Christmas)
Władzio (Vla-dzho)
Wujcio (Vuy-cho)—Uncle
Wy mordercy (Vi mor-der-tsy)—You murderers
Zaczekać (Za-che-kach)—Wait
Źegnajcie (Zheg-nye-chee)—Good-bye (farewell)
Zosia (Zo-sha)

Author's Note

To write or not to write was the question I asked myself before starting my memoirs. Did I want to bring back the past that I had tried so hard to erase from my memory for so many years? Did I want to relive all the painful events of my life?

My son told me, "Mom, the war is over—live in the present."

But my daughter said, "Please, Mom, I want to know about you. I want to preserve your writings for my children so that they know where their grandmother came from and why she is here in America."

I gathered up enough courage to sign up for a memoir-writing class at my local college. I didn't know what to expect. I wrote my first story like a diary. Dates and historical facts were important, but anyone could find those in history books. While all of my stories are historically accurate, I realized that I had to write about my feelings, impressions, fears, and joys of growing up as a prisoner on the steppes (dry, level grasslands) of Kazakhstan and as a refugee in the mountains and deserts of Persia and the jungles of Africa.

Memories flooded back before my eyes. I had to give them some coherence and shape.

Someone once asked me, "Did you keep a diary? How could you remember everything so well?"

I replied, "Those events were chiseled into my memory, and no matter how much I tried, I could never forget them."

Many times I was ready to give up. Recalling certain incidents was too painful, but, with tears rolling down my cheeks, I persevered.

As I wrote, many things became clear to me that I had not understood as a child. I saw that my mother—with her incredible strength, courage, determination, love, kindness, and, most of all, great sense of humor in the face of challenges and tragedies—was an inspiration to those who knew her. It was only through writing my stories that I realized how much she had done for my brother and me, and how many times her sacrifices saved our lives. She taught us that keeping faith and hope for the future can overcome despair and helplessness. Those who survived the war and overcame the obstacles leading to freedom emerged stronger, even though the emotional scars were hard to heal.

I decided to tell my story because it is not mine alone. It is the story of thousands of people who lost their homes and loved ones during the Second World War and were deported to Russia under the darkness of the night. It is a story that many historians refused to acknowledge, and that the Soviets tried to deny for many years.

Toward the end of my writing, I understood that I had a responsibility to keep those memories alive. Perhaps the legacy of my words will help keep history from repeating itself.

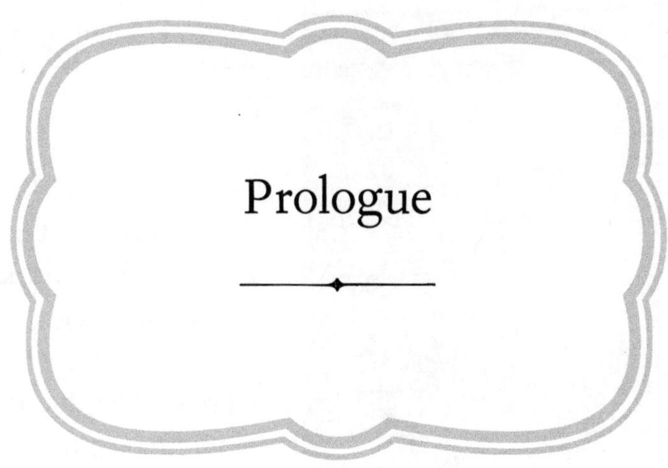

Prologue

Everybody calls me Krysia, which is the usual Polish nickname for Krystyna. I love my name—not because of how it sounds, but because it held such a happy memory for my parents.

My mother and father met at a ball in 1927. They danced the popular mazurka to a song called "Ostatni mazur" ("The Last Mazur") about a soldier asking a young girl named Krysia for one last dance before he goes off to war. "Pretty Krysia," go the words, "cease your weeping / Let us dance the mazur!" My parents fell in love that evening, dancing to that song. They married, and when I was born, on August 26, 1930, my father named me Krysia.

When I was a toddler, if I was crying, my father would pick me up and bounce me on his shoulder, singing,

My parents, Zofia and Andrzej Mihulka, were married in the late 1920s.

"Pretty Krysia, cease your weeping. Let us dance the mazurka!" I would laugh and clap my hands. When I grew older, he and I would dance together, hopping around the room. I learned the steps to the mazurka very early in my life.

Until I was nine and a half years old, I lived with my parents and my little brother, Antek, in the city of Lwów, then in southeastern Poland. I was not always very nice to my brother. It's not that I wouldn't play with him; I tried, but he was four years younger than me and too little to listen or understand anything. When I wanted him to act in plays with me (I loved to put on plays), he wouldn't cooperate. So I often got mad at him.

My father was the chief justice of an appellate court—the youngest judge to hold such a high position in Poland. My mother had degrees in chemistry and philosophy and even went to medical school for two years.

She enjoyed helping people and wanted to become a doctor, but her father hadn't allowed it. He loved her so much, he explained, that he was afraid she would catch a disease and die. Since he was paying for her studies, she had to obey him.

Our home was one in a row of houses attached to each other, with no gardens in front, just flowerpots at the entrances. The garden was at the back of each house. The bedrooms were upstairs, and downstairs were the living room, dining room, kitchen, and study.

When I was growing up Lwów was a city of more than 300,000 people. It was in the part of Poland that had been under Austrian occupation for 100 years before gaining its independence in 1918. Because of that, it had a distinct Austrian character; even the parks were fenced with elaborate stone carvings similar to the ones in Austria's capital city, Vienna. When we lived there, the main street, Leon Sapieha, was lined with all kinds of shops: clothing shops, china shops, and lots of bakeries. The largest bakery,

My brother, Antek, was four years younger than me.

the Wedel Café, had an indoor and an outdoor café and served mouthwatering French and Viennese pastries. My favorites were the chocolate éclairs—flaky pastries filled with creamy, delicious custard.

The Wedel Café was always full of gossiping friends. When I was eight years old the main topic was a man named Adolf Hitler. We heard Hitler's speeches on the radio every day. I hated hearing his voice—he was always shouting in a foreign language and sounded very angry. My mother told me he was speaking German, but I didn't know German, so I couldn't understand him. I did take French lessons from a private tutor who came once a week. I wasn't a very good student, because I only wanted to speak Polish. I remember seeing a photo of the two English princesses, Elizabeth and Margaret, in a magazine. Even though they didn't have any crowns and didn't look anything like the princesses in fairy tales, I was very interested in them because they were just about my age. But if I ever met them, I thought, I wouldn't even be able to talk to them, because they spoke English.

"Will I ever take English lessons?" I asked my mother.

"No, you'll never need to speak English," she answered. "As long as you can speak French and German, you can travel all over Europe. England is an island, and it's so far away."

I believed her. My mother was right about most things. Neither of us had any way of knowing how our lives would change or that, for most of my life, English would be my primary language.

PART I

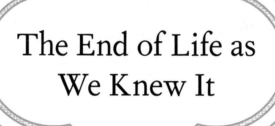

The End of Life as We Knew It

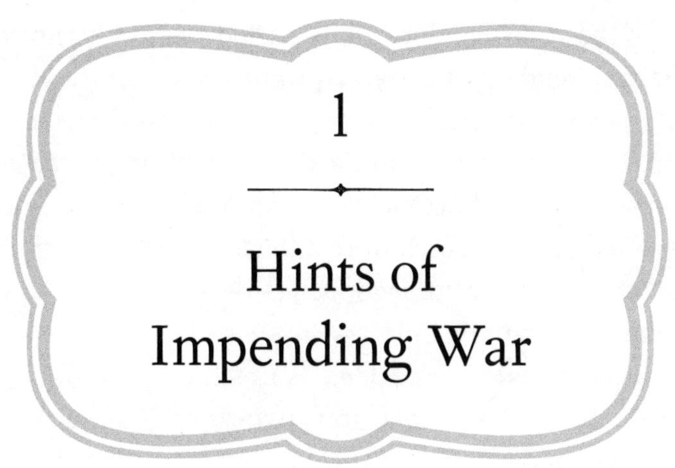

1

Hints of Impending War

It was the morning of March 12, 1938. I was seven and a half years old and eating breakfast with my family. Suddenly the music on the radio stopped and the announcer said, "Hitler has marched into Austria."

Both of my parents' faces fell.

"Tatusiu," I asked, "Is Hitler coming to Poland?"

"No, Krysiu, don't worry," my father answered, looking at my mother. I could tell that they didn't want to talk about it in front of me.

I picked up my lunch, kissed them each good-bye, and walked out to meet two of my friends, Marysia and Grażyna, for the short walk to school together.

My school, named Marii Magdalena, was only three blocks away, and when the weather was nice we always walked. Today the scent of tulips, violets, and daffodils from the street vendors' stalls drifted pleasantly through the air, sending the sweet promise of spring's arrival after a long winter. In the distance, against the blue sky, the Wysoki Zamek (Tall Castle) towered above the city. Centuries ago a fortress had been built there to defend the city. Now its ruins were a tourist attraction. In winter we pulled our little wooden sleds up to the castle and bounced down the hill.

I hated Marii Magdalena as much as I loved Lwów. The school was an old gray two-story building, with classrooms off the long corridors. Downstairs there was a recreation hall where we had morning prayers, assemblies, and, occasionally, school plays. Not only did I find school boring—except for gym class, where we had to climb ladders, which was terrifying—but I was also scared of the principal: short, stout Pani Morska, whose face reminded me of a bulldog. Her piercing pale-green eyes, hidden behind gray-rimmed glasses, took in every detail. Despite her unimpressive figure, she exerted a dictatorial air of authority. I tried to avoid her, but when I did pass her and had to say "*Dzień dobry.* Good day," my knees always started to shake. She would just stare at me. I never saw her smile.

"Why do you think she looks so mean?" I asked Marysia.

"I heard my mother tell my father that she's like that because she's an old maid."

"What does that have to do with anything?"

I enjoyed walking the streets of Lwów, sometimes with my father and Antek, sometimes with (below, from left) my mother and my aunts.

"Maybe she's angry because she didn't find a husband."

"How do you find a husband?" I asked.

"I don't know."

"My mother met my father at a ball, so I guess nobody ever asked Pani Morska to dance."

We lined up in the hallway as usual, before dispersing to our classrooms, but today a tall young man, wearing a very serious expression, stood next to Pani Morska and the teachers.

"Let me introduce Adam Kowalski from the Civil Defense organization," Pani Morska announced. "He is here to lecture us about the drills we will be having from time to time, in case of emergency."

Then Pan Kowalski spoke: "When you hear a siren, leave your classrooms immediately and run as fast as you can to trenches that will be dug in the field behind the school building. You will need to have masks to put over your faces in case of gas poisoning. Ask your parents to make masks for you. They should use gauze and cotton with elastic to hold it on around your head. When you reach the trenches, lie flat with your faces down until you are told to go back to school. Do not panic. Listen to your teachers' instructions. We hope that Hitler will not invade Poland, but we have to be prepared."

His words scared me. Could this really happen to us? I looked over at Marysia. She had a puzzled look on her face, as if she, too, were trying to understand if what Pan Kowalski said could ever come true. His words seemed unreal. They sounded like something I might read in one

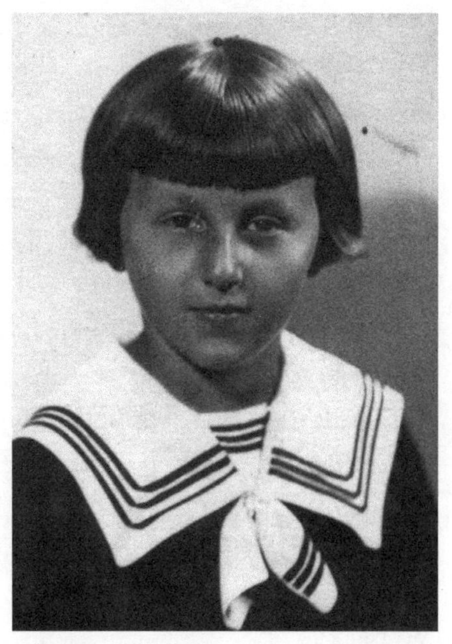

This formal portrait of me was taken before I had any understanding of how the war would affect my life.

of my father's history books, not like something that could ever be part of my life.

After Pan Kowalski's visit life went on its usual way, but things slowly began to feel different. On October 1 the announcement came that Hitler had invaded Sudetenland, a region of Czechoslovakia. After that, when we went to the Wedel Café, there seemed to be more and more people crowded inside, all talking about the possibility of war. I could feel tension in the air. On March 16, 1939, Hitler marched into Czechoslovakia, and my parents began discussing openly the need to stock food in the cellar and buy bags of sugar and flour.

One day at dinner I didn't want to eat what had been served. My father spoke to me sternly: "Eat, because one day you might want food but there won't be any." How was it possible not to have anything to eat? I wondered. Was that what the war was about?

My mother had made me a mask out of cotton, gauze, and elastic, as Pan Kowalski instructed, and I carried it to school every day. For a long time there were no drills. Then one day the wailing of a siren pierced the silence of the classroom, where we were doing arithmetic at our desks. We all jumped out of our seats and rushed to line up outside.

"Put on your masks!" one of the teachers shouted.

The newly dug trenches were a short distance from the building. We dropped down onto the soft ground, giggling and pushing each other. If this was war, then it was fun, I thought. Airplanes flew in circles above us, adding to the deafening sound. We stayed on the ground until the siren stopped and the teachers called, "Time to go back!"

When I got home that day, my mother said, "If the siren blows when we are home, then we all have to go down to the cellar. Will you remember that, Krysia?"

"Sure."

The radio was on, like always. Hitler's voice now sounded louder, rasping and ominous. It made me feel afraid, but I tried to shake off the fear. I was also filled with curiosity: What would the war really be like?

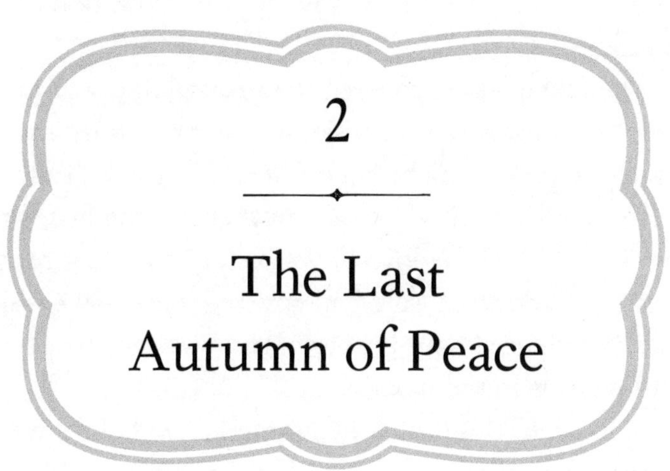

2

The Last Autumn of Peace

"Don't run so far that I won't be able to see you," shouted my mother.

"*Tak, Mamusiu!* Yes, Mommy, I hear you!" I called back. It was late September 1938; the air was cold and crisp, with a light wind rustling through the branches of the tall oak trees. This was the best time of year, I thought, before rainy and foggy November and then the endless snow and frost of the winter months. Antek and I were chasing each other in the park. A few screeching crows fought over bread crumbs somebody had left on a bench. The other birds had all flown to warmer climates. People of all ages strolled leisurely along the narrow paths in the park. Some led dogs that barked and pulled at their leashes. Voices and laughter carried across the park, adding to the happy and relaxed mood of the afternoon.

The fallen leaves covered the ground like a carpet of vibrant colors: rusty burnt sienna, dark red, mustard yellow, olive green, and bright orange. Antek and I rolled in them, having fun, while our mother watched us, smiling. I could feel the love flowing out of her big brown eyes. A dark-green felt hat covered her wavy, shiny chestnut-colored hair. I thought she was the most beautiful woman in the world.

"Children, time to gather some leaves before we go home," she called. We ran to her, and she gave us two little baskets she had brought along.

I picked through the cold, damp leaves, choosing only the best-looking ones. Different shapes and sizes soon filled my basket. Antek, being only four, was slower, and I wanted to offer to help, but I knew he liked to do it himself.

My mother looked at her watch. "It's almost four o'clock, and your father will be coming home for dinner. Let's go."

"Can we please have some Penguin ice cream on the way?" I asked.

"Only if you promise to eat your dinner."

"We will, we will!"

We walked out of the park, into the street. The last rays of the sun were still lingering, but dusk was approaching. Passing tramcars made clicking sounds, and one-horse carriages waited for passengers by the sidewalk.

Antek poses proudly with his new tricycle for this formal portrait.

Soon we reached a kiosk where soda water, chocolate and lemon wafers, and ice cream were sold. A big poster of a penguin hung on the door of the kiosk. Penguin ice cream—vanilla ice cream on a stick, covered with chocolate—was the latest novelty from Warsaw, Poland's capital. I loved its sweet flavor, which tasted better than any homemade concoction.

When we got home I put the leaves I had collected between pages of heavy books so they would dry. Later I would take them out and play with them, arranging them into different patterns.

Soon enough the glorious autumn was gone and winter set in. In spite of the cold, I loved December because of its two holidays: Saint Nicholas Day on December 6 and Christmas. Saint Nicholas was especially exciting because of all the gifts. All Polish children knew that after we went to sleep on December 5, Saint Nicholas would sneak into our homes and leave us presents. When we woke up the morning of the sixth, there they were! The year before I had pretended to be asleep so I could see Saint Nicholas, but instead I saw my mother sneak into my room and arrange all the presents on my bed! I was shocked, but I knew better than to tell her what I had seen. I was afraid I wouldn't get presents anymore if I told.

When I woke up on Saint Nicholas Day this year, there were crayons and books for me— I loved to draw and paint and read. (My favorite days were the ones when I didn't have to go to school but could stay home and read by myself.) Sometimes I also got a doll on Saint

Nicholas Day, but not this year. The one thing I—and most Polish children—always got was a red velvet devil. The size of the devil depended on how good or bad you had been during the year. I had a really big one this year because I hadn't been nice enough to my brother.

Since Saint Nicholas brought gifts earlier in the month, Christmas was not much of a gift-giving occasion. We just had small presents under the tree—little boxes of chocolates or candies, maybe an exotic orange. The fun part of Christmas was decorating the tree the day before. Ciocia Tocha, my mother's youngest sister, came to help; we wrapped candies, chocolates, and homemade gingerbread cookies in colorful papers. On one end of each paper wrapper we tied a piece of wool thread and made a loop so we could hang the candy on the tree. In the days after Christmas, we ate all the goodies off the tree! We carefully placed small candles in little holders that clipped to the tree branches. When the candles were lit, the room turned magical. I thought our tree this year, with all its trimmings, was the most beautiful one we had ever had. Maybe I remember it as so beautiful because it was the last one we ever had in our home.

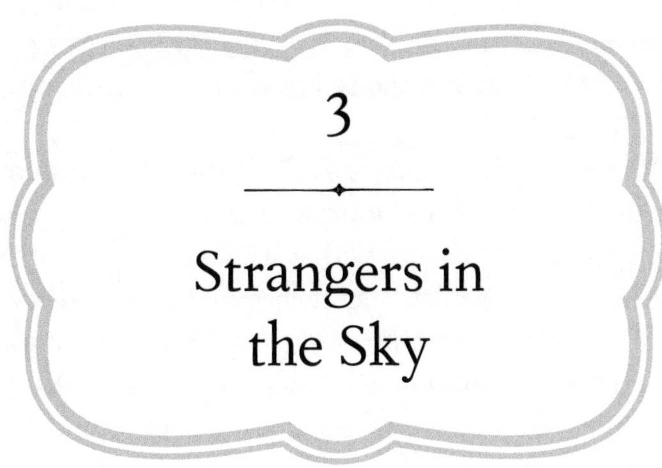

3

Strangers in the Sky

September 1, 1939, started just like any other day. My father left for court, my mother went out on some errands, and Antek and I stayed at home with Mila, our beloved nanny and housekeeper. Autumn had barely begun, so school hadn't started yet.

"Krysiu, Antek," Mila called. "We are leaving for the park by 11 o'clock. Get ready."

I couldn't wait to go. I was eager to start gathering a collection of colorful leaves to press and dry.

At about 11 o'clock we left the house and walked to the kiosk at the corner, where we stopped for some sparkling lemonade. An electric tram passed us and came to a stop nearby. A one-horse carriage carrying two passengers made a clicking noise on the cobblestone street.

A crowd was gathered around the kiosk, discussing the latest news about the war everybody knew was coming with Germany. Nobody knew just when, or how, it would begin.

The roaring sound of airplanes broke the tranquility of the peaceful scene. I looked up and saw five low-flying, dark-colored shapes with a strange sign resembling a broken cross painted on each one. I heard someone say, "Our pilots are training—getting ready for the war." I thought they did not look like Polish airplanes, but children were not supposed to voice their opinions to grown-ups, so I kept quiet.

Suddenly a loud explosion reverberated in the air.

"Bombs, bombs!" someone shouted.

"Boże, zlituj się! God have mercy!" another voice wailed.

The crowd dispersed in a panic. Mila grabbed Antek and shouted, *"Szybko, szybko, lećmy do domu!* Quick, quick, hurry home!"

We rushed home. I had never seen Mila run so fast; I could barely keep up with her.

We should have gone right to the cellar, but we were too curious, so instead we ran upstairs to look out the windows. From our windows, I could see the Polish army's military training base up on a hill. The tall gray buildings were visible against the cloudless blue sky. I watched as the planes flew over them, and I saw bombs falling. The sound was deafening, louder than when we were on the street. I dropped to the floor, covering my ears, shaking and crying. Antek screamed and held onto Mila.

Mila tried to calm us. "Don't be afraid. Soon it will be over."

I heard the wailing of the warning siren. Why did it start so late?

I looked again out the window at the military buildings, but, to my amazement, they were gone. Instead, a ball of fire met my eyes. The planes had vanished as quickly as they had come.

A few hours later my mother came home. She was pale and looked very upset. She grabbed Antek and me and held us closely, exclaiming, "You're okay! You're okay! I was so worried—so many people were killed today. Germany attacked us without declaring war, and without any warning. When the next attack comes," she instructed, "we must all go down to the cellar."

"Mamusiu," I asked, "The planes had a strange sign painted on them. What was it?"

"They are swastikas, the symbol of the Nazi Party. Hitler is their leader."

I knew who Hitler was. He was the man who was always screaming on the radio.

My mother was trained as a Red Cross volunteer for a block of houses on our street. She put a white band with a red cross on her arm and packed her first aid kit. She gave each of us a mask in case of a poisonous gas attack and showed us how to use them. They were the same kind she had made for me to take to school. Then she gave us a warning: "Children, do not pick up any toys or candy lying on the street or in the garden. Germans are known to drop poisonous ones from the planes."

I didn't understand. Why would anybody want to poison children?

We started getting ready to live in the cellar, which was to be our bomb shelter. My mother and Mila gathered pillows, blankets, canned food, and dry biscuits. I was nine, and Antek wasn't even five yet, but we helped by packing toys. I was given a small bench against the wall to sleep on, and my brother would sleep in his stroller. My mother and Mila would share an old sofa that stood in the middle of the cellar.

We carried everything down the narrow stairs. It was dark and damp in the candlelit cellar. Sharp odors from a large barrel of sauerkraut and from a smaller one of pickled cucumbers filled the air. Shelves packed with jars of home-canned peaches, apricots, and strawberry jam lined the walls. A sandbox, filled with potatoes and apples stored for the coming winter, took up a lot of the floor space.

Awaiting my father, we went back upstairs. When he came in he was accompanied by his brother, my *wujcio* Tomek, and a family friend. Without greeting us, they locked themselves in the study. I stood near the door, trying to eavesdrop, but I couldn't hear anything they said.

When they finally emerged, their faces were sad. My father explained to Antek and me that he and my uncle were reservists in the Polish army. That meant they had to report for duty now that the country had been attacked. He turned to my mother and said with emotion, "Please, take care of yourselves." Then he turned to Antek and me. "Children, obey your mother."

They embraced us and were gone.

My mother tried to hide the tears in her eyes, but I could see them. I was distressed at my father's leaving, and afraid of what would happen next. Antek played happily with his toy horse on wheels, not understanding the seriousness of the situation.

A few days later the Germans attacked Lwów and the fighting began. Whenever the siren sounded we would rush to the cellar. The electricity was cut off, but luckily we still had water. Between the air raids we could go upstairs to wash. When we did, we could hear the bullets whistling outside.

Sitting in the dark cellar for hours every day, breathing in the smell of sauerkraut and pickled cucumbers, made me long to breathe fresh air and see the sky. After about a week, I couldn't bear it any longer. Without asking permission, I sneaked up the cellar stairs to the door that led into the small garden at the back of the house. I felt safe there. I breathed in the early autumn air. The leaves were blowing off the trees, covering the ground in brown, yellow, and purple. I had just bent down to pick up the ones I liked best when something whistled past my ear. I froze. I knew instantly. A bullet.

Shaking, I ran into the house. My mother was frantic. "Where did you go?" She noticed the two leaves in my hand. "How could you go outside? Promise never to do that again!"

"I promise, I promise," I whispered meekly. I didn't tell her about the bullet. Had I not bent to pick up the leaves, I could have been shot. Maybe the leaves saved my life.

Finally, one morning all was quiet. Mila went out, and when she returned she had several leaflets, which had been dropped by a German plane. "All women and children should leave the city by 4 PM," my mother read. After that time, the city was to be destroyed.

It was up to my mother to make a decision. Her face was pale and worried. She sat down on the sofa in the cellar and held us close. Finally, she spoke, in a decisive voice.

"If we stay here, we will die, but at least we will die in our own home. We are not leaving."

Soon after four o'clock the bombing started again, louder and stronger than before. We wore our masks in case of a poisonous gas attack. Jars of canned food began falling off the shelves. The air was full of dust from the walls. My mother held Antek closely; he was crying. I grabbed Mila's skirt. "Trust in God," my mother tried to comfort us.

I was terrified, but tried not to show it. My body was tense, my heart was beating quickly, and I wanted to scream, but no sounds came out. I remembered what my father once told me: "In the face of danger, be brave. Only the weak show fear." Easier said than done, I thought now.

After what seemed like an eternity, the bombing stopped. We climbed out of the cellar. Our house still stood, although half of the roof had been destroyed. Glass from broken windows was everywhere, but we were alive.

The next morning all was quiet again; there were no bombs and no whistling bullets. My mother said, "That's strange. It's the 10th day of the invasion, but I don't see any Germans moving in. Our Polish soldiers must be good fighters."

Later that day my father came home, still in uniform. He looked tired, and his usually smiling eyes had lost their twinkle. We ran to him, and he embraced us.

"Children, children, I am so glad to see that you are safe! It's a good thing you didn't walk out of the house yesterday. I heard that those who left their homes were bombed on the road and did not survive." He turned to my mother. "You made the right decision. It was very brave of you."

My mother smiled in reply and put her arms around my father. Then she asked, "But why are you here and not with the army?"

"The Germans are retreating. I was dismissed, but nobody told me why. Let's listen to the radio."

The announcement came as soon as we turned on the radio. "The Polish government has surrendered. The battle for Poland has been lost." Then everything went silent.

"Where are the Germans?" my mother wondered aloud. "Why didn't they occupy the city?"

Wujcio Tomek arrived. He was taller than my father, with chestnut hair and a suntanned face. I loved him

This is one of the last pictures taken of my family together. We had no idea that we would soon be separated, or of the suffering and tragedy that we would come to endure.

because he always let me stand on one of his legs while he swung me back and forth. He also laughed a lot.

Today there was no smile on his face. He told us, "I heard from my commanding officer that the Russians are taking over our part of Poland."

My parents looked shocked. "Why? How is this possible?"

My uncle continued, "I've learned that on August 23, Hitler and Russian leader Joseph Stalin signed a secret treaty called Ribbentrop-Molotov. They became allies and divided Poland between themselves."

Everybody was silent. Finally, my father said quietly, "That's unbelievable. We have no idea what to expect next."

I listened carefully, growing more confused with every word I heard.

That night I was happy to be sleeping in my bed again, but in the middle of the night strange noises woke me. I got up and looked out the window but didn't see anybody outside. The noise turned into a roaring, which grew louder and louder. Soon I saw tanks rolling and soldiers marching. The gas lamps on the street were broken, but the moon shone brightly, illuminating the silhouettes of the invading enemy. The Russians were coming, their boots striking the pavement with the sound of approaching doom.

I stood petrified, my heart pounding.

My mother walked in. "Don't look out anymore. Just pray and go to sleep."

I couldn't sleep. The noises continued, and the fear would not leave me.

I wondered, What will happen next?

4

Life Under Russian Occupation

The Russians took over the radio. They announced that they had come as friends, to save us from the Germans. They sounded like they expected us to be grateful. But the only people who were happy about the Russians being in Poland were the Polish Communists, who offered their services to help them.

My mother's sister Stefa lived in Lwów, too, with her husband, Władzio, and her two daughters, Zosia and Nina. During our family gatherings I often listened to Wujcio Władzio's stories about being taken prisoner by the Russians during the First World War. He would describe what life was like during the three years he was held captive in Siberia and how he escaped to Poland by hiding on freight and cattle trains. I was fascinated by his stories and remembered most of them.

One day soon after the Russians invaded, Ciocia Stefa came over, crying. She said, "Władzio does not want to get out of bed. He cries like a baby and tells us that he sees us all in Siberia. Please come and talk some sense into him." My mother agreed to go talk to my uncle and told me to come with her. We left Antek home with Mila.

When we got there my uncle was still in bed, just like my aunt had said. "What's wrong with you?" My mother asked him. "So far the Russians are behaving very well toward us. Isn't it better that they are here, instead of the Germans?"

We were very close with the family of my mother's sister Stefa, seen here on a family vacation with her husband, Władzio, and my two older cousins, Zosia (right, in white) and Nina.

"You don't know them!" my uncle replied. "Wait a little longer and you will see what they are like. They will destroy us. Under Communism, everything belongs to the state. We will not be permitted to own anything. Even our souls will belong to them, as they will not allow us to worship and will turn our churches into stables for horses."

The discussion continued, but I lost interest. I walked out onto the bedroom balcony that overlooked the garden at the back of the house. In the adjoining garden, I saw two of my school friends. The balcony's decorative railings were too high for me to lean over, and I wanted to talk to my friends. I pushed my head through the narrow opening between the two iron rods.

"Ewa, Danusia, I'm here visiting my uncle," I shouted over to them. "Can you come over to my house tomorrow to play?"

"We'll ask our mothers and let you know," they called back.

Then I heard my mother's voice: "Come, Krysiu. We're going home now."

"In a minute, Mamusiu." I tried to pull my head out from between the railings, but couldn't. I panicked.

"Help!" I screamed. "Get me out of here!"

My mother and my aunt rushed out to the balcony. They tried to pull my head out, but to no avail. The railings held me in a tight grip.

"What shall we do?" wailed my mother. "Shall we call somebody to cut the railings?"

"Calm down," replied Ciocia Stefa. "I'll get some cream, or even lard if necessary." She disappeared for a moment, and when she came back she smeared some cream on my neck, my ears, and the railings. She and my mother took turns massaging me until they could pull out one ear. Then they worked on the second one, and when it slipped out, the rest of my head was free.

"How on earth did you manage to get your head in there in the first place?" scolded my mother.

"I don't know. I won't do it again. I've learned my lesson."

After my unfortunate adventure, which left me with a stiff neck and purple bruises, my mother and I headed home, leaving my uncle wallowing in his despair.

The government offices and schools were closed. A few small shops remained open, but after the German bombing and fighting around the city, there was not much left for sale.

One day the Russians announced that the judicial and police services had to be restored. They asked everybody to report to work. My father went to court. A short time later he was back. He looked rushed and upset.

"I was walking down the long entrance hall," he told us, "and as I was about to enter the courtroom, Ludwik, the janitor, stopped me and said, 'Do not go in—you will not come out.' I turned around and left as fast as I could. I have to go into hiding. I am on the wanted list."

My mother began to cry.

My father threw some clothing into a small suitcase and embraced each of us. "I will come to see you from time to time," he promised. And then he was gone.

My father was of medium height, with light-green eyes and brown hair and a kind smile that attracted others to him. He had helped many people find jobs, including Ludwik, the janitor who warned him of the danger he was in that day.

We learned later, through Wujcio Władzio—who did not go to court as instructed—that the five judges and six lawyers who did go into the courtroom that morning had been arrested, and had disappeared. He said they were probably sent to Siberia, or executed. Later, many more lawyers, policemen, and army officers were rounded up and taken away.

Wujcio Władzio had been right. The Russians were starting to show their true faces.

The schools reopened, too. I was in fourth grade, but my mother didn't let me go to school. I wondered why, but was afraid to ask. I had a feeling that it had something to do with the Russians and that my mother didn't want to frighten me. She always tried to protect me by not telling me the whole story. But one day I heard her talking to her friend Pani Lusia, who was visiting. I sat nearby pretending to play with my dolls, but listening attentively. My mother told Pani Lusia she had heard a rumor that children would be taken away from the schools and sent to orphanages to be brought up as good Communists. Nobody paid any attention to me as I continued pretending to play quietly while an image of me alone among strangers flashed through my mind and filled me with a new fear.

Soon a letter arrived from school, asking about my absence. A friend who was a doctor responded, as a favor to my mother, explaining that I was disabled and would receive tutoring at home. I couldn't believe it; my mother had taught me never to tell lies, and here she was lying for me. Life was bringing more and more surprises—and most of them not good ones—every day.

Luckily my friends were able to visit me, and I was allowed to go to their houses, too, so we could still have fun playing with each other. Some of my friends' parents also found good excuses and made up lies for the authorities so they could keep their children home from school.

One day there was a loud knocking at our front door. "Open up and let us in," a deep voice shouted.

Mila opened the door, and there, in the bright light of the afternoon sun, stood two NKVD officers (Russian security) and a militia interpreter.

"We need accommodations for the army officers and their families," the interpreter said to us in Polish.

My mother appeared, looking very pale. My knees shook as I followed her and the soldiers around the house. "We will take the lower part" (which included the living room, dining room, and study), said one of the NKVD through the interpreter, "and leave you the bedrooms upstairs and access to the kitchen downstairs."

A few days later a young couple with a nine-month-old baby moved into our downstairs rooms. The officer was tall, blond, and handsome, and his wife was also blonde, with lovely blue eyes and a pleasant, kind expression. They were rather shy and very poor. The man wore his uniform, but the woman was dressed shabbily in a brown dress that didn't fit her, a gray jacket, and a straw hat. Her shoes were very worn, and she had no stockings or socks, even though it was quite cold by this time in October. The baby was wrapped in a blanket. They had no suitcases; instead they carried their belongings in two beige canvas bags.

We were upset that our privacy had been invaded, but we also felt sorry for them. It was hard to communicate, but through their gestures, we understood they needed baths. My mother took the woman upstairs and lit the gas water heater to start the bath. We heard the woman scream, and then she ran downstairs. My mother followed, laughing. "She thought I was going to kill her when she saw the flames shoot up. I guess she has never seen a bathtub with a gas water heater."

Katia, which we later learned was her name, would never again ask to take a bath. Instead she would heat water in a big kettle in the kitchen and then carry it to a tin-plated bowl set in the middle of the living room, where the three of them slept.

Always curious, I often peeped through the half-open door to see how they were living in our rooms. I was horrified to find that their pantry full of food supplies was on top of our long black piano. I would certainly not be able to practice piano anymore!

Even though they were not a frightening family, after they moved in I felt afraid to be alone. I started sleeping with my mother in her bed; Antek's crib was next to us. It felt better that we were all together at night.

We were not the only people in the city whose houses were occupied by Russian families. When my mother's friend Pani Lusia came to visit again, she said, "Do you know what happened in my home? The officer who lives with us came to me this morning with wet hair and complained that our sinks were too low and he had to kneel to wash his hair. It turns out he washed his hair in the toilet!" My mother, Pani Lusia, and I all burst out laughing. Even living in fear, with our homes invaded, had its comic moments.

Christmas was coming. The stores were empty, but the local open-air market was full of people bringing eggs, chickens, and vegetables from the countryside in horse-drawn carts. There wasn't as much as usual because the Russians needed to feed the army and each farm had to supply them with a certain amount of food.

The day before Christmas Mila returned home from her trip to the market empty-handed and very upset. "I couldn't buy anything," she told us, "because nobody would accept my money. People around me were in a panic and swearing at the Russians." Mila explained that when she asked somebody what was going on, she was told that our Polish złoty no longer had any value. Only Russian rubles would be accepted for purchases. "How are we going to buy food for Christmas?" she moaned. "What are we going to do?"

"This is catastrophic," my mother said, trying to be calm. "But we will find a solution. I will go to my sister Stefa and find out what she knows. We'll find a way to raise some money."

I listened carefully but couldn't quite understand. I knew that the Russians were trying to spoil our Christmas, but I didn't comprehend the seriousness and consequences of devaluing the Polish złoty. Still, I could tell that the news was really bad.

My mother came back from Ciocia Stefa's with a solution. "The Russians have no shoes and only rags for clothes. We are going to sell them our clothes and shoes, and then we will have rubles to buy the food we need."

My mother, Mila, and I carried our clothing in small bags to the market where the farmers sold their produce. Now it was bustling with city sellers like us. We found whatever space we could and pulled out our dresses, skirts, blouses, and shoes, and bargained with the Russians. "Ten rubles," Mila would say to an interested Russian, showing her ten fingers. "*Nyet, nyet,*" the Russian would reply, and display eight fingers. Mila would then spread out nine fingers. If the Russian agreed, the deal was closed to the satisfaction of both parties.

These were my first lessons in the Russian language. Sometimes the Russian would say, "*Nyetu deneg.* No money." Some sellers screamed out prices in Polish and then wondered why the Russians, who understood no Polish, walked away.

My mother hated the noise and the crowds, but I enjoyed the excitement of haggling. It was much more fun than going to school. And although I was not being formally educated, my experience on the black market proved to be quite valuable later in life.

From time to time my father risked his life by visiting us. He would slip into the house silently, after it was dark, taking the chance that the residing Russian family would not notice. Perhaps they did, but we were lucky because they never reported him.

One March evening, as he was leaving after one of his short visits, he took me aside. With a serious expression, he said, "Krysiu, if anything ever happens to me, promise to take care of your brother and help your mother."

"What could happen to you?" I asked, trying not to show the fear that suddenly gripped me.

He didn't reply, just looked at me sadly. Then he kissed each of us and was gone.

My mother tried to cheer me up. "Once the war is over everything will go back to normal," she said.

I wanted to believe her but couldn't shake off my growing fear of the future.

When I was a little girl, I loved sitting on my father's lap. I missed him terribly when he had to go into hiding.

5

Shadows in the Night

Somebody was ringing the front-door bell. The sound woke me up. I looked at the clock on the wall: Seven in the morning? Who would be visiting so early?

Then I heard the front door open and steps coming up to the bedroom. My mother and Ciocia Stefa walked in. I pretended to be asleep, but opened my eyes from time to time.

My mother spoke very quietly, but I could hear her. "Stefa, Stefa, what are you doing here so early? Did something happen?"

Ciocia Stefa was sobbing as she tried to speak, and her voice sounded frantic. "They arrested Władzio last night. He tried to escape through the back door, but the soldiers had surrounded the house."

"The Russians came to arrest Jędruś, too." I had to strain to hear my mother, who was whispering now. "But, of course, he wasn't here. They were quiet and didn't wake the children up. Then they threw everything out of the closets and drawers and left without taking anything. I am going to start packing today; by Sunday we will leave Lwów and go to Hala's. We will change our names. If you want, you can come with us."

Ciocia Hala, my mother's oldest sister, lived in the town of Drochobycz. She had beautiful blue eyes and golden hair. I used to call her an angel. I loved her very much.

"I can't think clearly right now," Ciocia Stefa said through her tears. "I will let you know. *Do widzenia.* Good-bye." I slit open my eyes in time to see my mother and aunt embrace. Then my aunt was gone.

When I got out of bed a few minutes later, I saw clothing, purses, and shoes on the floor. My mother's face grew worried as she saw me taking in the scene, but she tried to sound cheerful. "I'm cleaning because we are moving soon."

"Fine, Mamusiu, I will help you pack." Uncharacteristically, I decided not to ask any questions, and my mother did not offer any more information.

Thursday night I was sleeping peacefully when I suddenly felt someone shaking my arm.

"Wake up, Krysiu. You have to get up."

I opened my eyes to see our neighbor Pani Alina, an elderly woman, bending over me. Next to her, next to my bed, stood a Russian soldier, yellow-skinned, with slanted eyes and a vacant expression, his bayonet fixed on me.

I pulled the bedcovers over my head, hoping the nightmare would disappear.

But it was not a dream. Pani Alina forced the blanket off my face. "Krysiu, I will help you dress. Get up, get up!"

I opened my eyes again and tried to move, but I was so scared I couldn't. I started shaking violently, my teeth chattering. The soldier did not move. I noticed Antek sitting in his crib, looking confused while Mila, sobbing loudly over him, tried to dress him.

Where was my mother?

Then I heard her screaming in the next room, "You are going to shoot us!"

"No, no," a man's voice replied.

Pani Alina gently helped me out of bed and started pulling layers of clothing onto me. The soldier finally lowered his bayonet and walked into the other room.

My legs felt weak, but I had to find out what was going on. I went into my father's library, which was filled with Russian soldiers. All of his leather-bound books had been thrown off the shelves onto the floor. The soldiers were poking them with bayonets. A few dried leaves had fallen out of the pages of some of the books and were being crumbled by the soldiers' feet. I realized these were the beautiful leaves I had collected that last peaceful autumn of 1938 and placed in those books to dry.

What were the Russians looking for? My father was a kind man who always helped people. Why would they suspect him of doing anything wrong? I was afraid of the soldiers, but they just glanced at me and then ignored me as I passed into the next room.

Here, in a bedroom that had been converted into our dining room, my mother was sitting at the table opposite a Russian officer. The room was filled with soldiers and strange men who, I found out later, were Polish militia and interpreters, Communists collaborating with the Russians. The officer was writing something down, and a Polish collaborator sat next to him, translating my mother's words. I heard them asking my mother about my father and her telling them she didn't know where he was, didn't have his address. The officer turned to me and said something in Russian, which I didn't understand. I thought I noticed a flicker of emotion—pity, perhaps—in his eyes as he looked at me. Maybe I reminded him of his own children? Maybe it was my imagination, but as we stared at each other I thought that he probably hated what he had to do, that he was acting on orders, and that he felt sorry for me, an innocent victim of these dreadful circumstances.

"We will take you to see your father," the interpreter told me. But if they didn't know where he was, how could they do that? I realized he was lying. Where were they going to take us? Why did we have to leave our house?

I ran into my bedroom and looked at my dollhouse, with its miniature brown wooden furniture and red velvet-covered sofa. My most cherished possession, a golden painted china tea set, was displayed on a shelf above a large doll bed where my favorite doll, the one that looked like Shirley Temple, lay. I lifted her out of bed and pressed her against my face. Suddenly a Polish militiaman was there, grabbing her away from me. He threw the doll on the floor and shouted, "You do not need dolls where you are going! There everybody works for the benefit of the nation and there is no time for foolish play!"

I didn't want to go to a place where children were not free to behave like children. I didn't want to know the world he was describing. Thoughts of escape leapt into my mind. I moved toward an open window. It was then that I noticed, in the dim light of the streetlamp, outlines of more soldiers with bayonets fixed on the house, surrounding us. There was no way out.

Katia, the Russian woman living in our house with her baby and officer husband, appeared and began to help us pack. She was a kind woman, and we had always had a good relationship. She found some tin-plated mugs we used on picnics and some string, and tied the mugs together around our necks. I didn't understand why she was doing this, but I let her.

The officer in charge stood up. "*Poshli.*"

"Time to go," the interpreter announced.

My mother walked into her bedroom, and we all followed. A replica of an oil painting by Flemish painter

Peter Paul Rubens of Madonna and Child hung over her bed. The Madonna's eyes were gazing steadily at us. My mother knelt down and prayed: "Oh God, please have mercy on us and save us! Do not desert us in our hour of need."

The militiaman laughed. "*Zduriwa, zduriwa*. She has gone crazy," he said.

I didn't pray. Where *was* God, anyway? I had been taught that God loved little children, and yet He was letting these wicked men throw us out of our home. Why didn't God come to our rescue? Did the Russians have more power than God? I blamed Him for what was happening to us. Or could I be wrong? Did my mother know something about God that I didn't know?

The Russian officer picked up Antek and started walking toward the door. Mila screamed, "*Wy mordercy!* You murderers!" but the Russians paid no attention. My mother followed the officer, and I followed her. Mila and Pani Alina came, too, carrying our bags. Katia disappeared.

We walked through the kitchen, where the floor was covered with flour and sugar, which were flowing out of the pierced burlap bags. Then we went through the hallway, out the door, into the street and the darkness of the cold April night. It was well past midnight, so it was already Friday. Friday the 13th, 1940.

A truck was waiting, and my mother and I climbed up into it, as instructed. The officer, still holding Antek, sat next to the driver and placed my brother on his knee.

I looked at the neighboring houses and thought I saw drapes moving and obscure shadows peering out at us.

Mila tried to climb onto the truck with us, but one of the Russian soldiers grabbed her and pushed her off. The Polish militiaman shouted, "You stupid woman! Your life is just beginning. We are getting rid of the bourgeois rich. This world now belongs to the working class."

I knew that Mila did not agree. She was an orphan, and now she was losing her home, her job, and the only people who cared for her.

The truck shook and started moving away. I looked back at the house. The door was still open, and Mila and Pani Alina were visible against the light coming from the inside. Soon the view of our house merged into the dim line of dwellings and I couldn't make it out anymore.

We passed along the streets of Lwów that were so familiar and dear to me, but I noticed the shadows of Russian soldiers guarding trucks in front of many of the houses. I heard shrieks and cries of despair and could picture the same things that we had just been through happening in those homes.

I could smell the fresh spring air. It made me think of the Easter processions going through the streets, of flower vendors selling violets and irises, of people laughing and ladies parading in their new spring clothes and fashionable hats. There was no laughter on these streets tonight.

I felt trapped, like an animal being driven to the slaughterhouse. I had read about the French Revolution and remembered how the prisoners were led to the guillotines. My mother held me tight next to her, and we were silent. There were no words that could express our emotions.

We arrived at the railway station. The black forms of cattle wagons loomed in front of us. A door opened on one of the wagons, and the silent Russian guards pushed us into the darkness on the other side. The locks clicked with a loud bang. I could feel the presence of other people and hear movements, cries, and prayers. I sat on my suitcase and wished I could disappear into some other life.

Morning came. Rays of light penetrated the small windows high above. Faces became visible, and cries of surprise filled the air as friends and neighbors recognized each other.

I saw two rows of bunks standing against opposite sides of the wagon. A curtain hung in the middle, covering a hole that served as a toilet.

I heard someone calling me. "Krysiu, Krysiu, it's Marysia. Grażyna is here, too."

My two friends with whom I used to walk to school every morning were sitting nearby. I tried to smile but could only nod my head in reply. My mother and Grażyna's mother embraced each other, crying.

The door opened with a clatter, and cold air rushed into the wagon. Three NKVD men wearing green uniforms came in. An interpreter in civilian clothing accompanied them.

"*Familia* Mihulka!" one of the men called.

My mother walked over and sat on a trunk in the middle of the wagon, facing the Russians.

"Where is your husband?"

"I don't know."

"What was his profession?"

"He was an accountant," my mother lied.

"Was he in the Polish army?"

"No, he was not in the Polish army," she lied again. I couldn't believe my mother was telling all these lies, she who had always taught me to tell the truth. I knew she must have a reason; she must know something I didn't.

One by one, other names were called, and the interrogations continued. Why were the Russians so curious about our lives? Why did they arrest us? I didn't understand anything that was going on.

The NKVD left, and two soldiers brought in a bucket of cabbage soup and jugs of water. Now I understood why Katia had tied the mugs around our necks.

"*Kushayte!* Eat!" one of the soldiers called as they banged the door behind them on the way out.

"Pani Mihulka, where are you?" a voice was calling outside.

"Mila, it's Mila!" my mother exclaimed. She grabbed Antek and hurriedly climbed up one of the bunks to the window. She tried to push Antek out through the small opening, shouting to Mila, "Take him, take him and give him to the family!"

We heard a guard outside chase Mila away from the train, and heard her sobbing. My mother covered her face and cried.

The train whistle blew. The train started moving slowly, and as it gained speed, the rattling noise of the creaking wagons became louder and louder. Our journey into captivity had begun.

PART II

Journey into Captivity

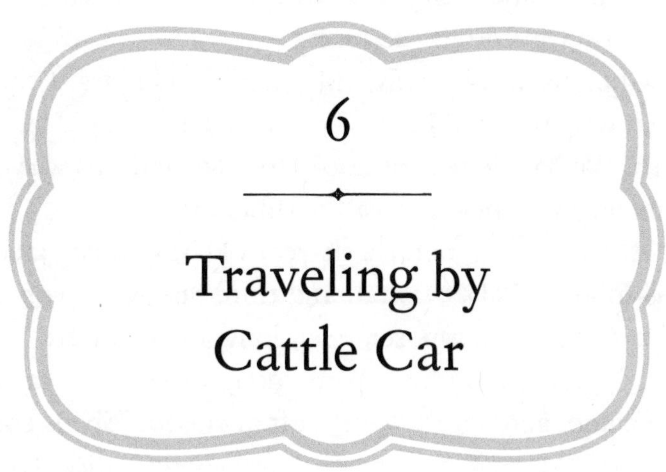

6

Traveling by Cattle Car

Space in the wagon was very limited, and access to the windows, which were by the upper bunks, difficult. Everybody agreed to take turns by the windows to get a view of the passing scenery.

Whenever we arrived at a station, our train drove onto the middle railway tracks. There we were hidden from the platforms by trains on either side of us so that any people standing on the platforms wouldn't see us. Guards armed with rifles paced along both sides of our train, their boots striking the pavement with a sound that warned escape was impossible.

The cattle car was airless and dark. The intolerable crowding prevented movement. Most of the time we had to sit huddled together. During the days on the train my friends and I played a word game. Marysia would say, "It starts with the letter *b*."

Grażyna would reply, "My name is Barbara. I come from Bulgaria, and I carry beans." Then it would be my turn. We had no toys or books to read, and this was the only way we knew to pass the time.

Antek made a friend, a six-year-old boy named Janek. His mother, Lala, was tall and thin. She was a concert pianist and a composer. Her long fingers were constantly moving on her lap, as though she were playing the piano, and her eyes were often closed. "She is composing," Marysia whispered. Everybody called Lala's mother Babcia (Granny); she was the one who mostly looked after Janek.

There was also Pani Irena, a young and pretty woman with large blue eyes and long blonde hair, which she tied back with a bow. Her two little girls, Ewa and Danusia, were three and five years old. Her husband was an army officer and had been arrested when the Russians marched into Poland.

Each night I tried to sleep to the constant, deafening sound of squeaking wheels and whistling wind, which penetrated the thin walls of the moving wagon. I dreamed of my lost home. I missed my father. With each stop, I was jerked awake. I heard the names of the stations we passed through: Kiev, Moscow, Omsk, Novosibirsk. I heard people talking: "We have crossed the Ural Mountains—we are in Asia." I lost count of the days and nights. Nobody could guess where we were going. Nobody had any maps.

One day, when we were at a station, the door opened and a Russian soldier ordered, "Four people come out to get water." I saw people from the other wagons marching under the watchful eyes of the soldiers. Suddenly my heart leapt: I saw Ciocia Stefa and my cousins, Zosia and Nina, walking with the crowd.

I screamed to my mother, "They're here!"

"Who? Who is here?" My mother managed to push her way toward the open door. And then she also recognized them.

"Stefa! Stefa!" she cried.

Ciocia Stefa and my cousins looked up, stunned. Then Ciocia Stefa shouted, "We will be together!" A Russian soldier pushed them to keep moving.

I stood still, in shock, then looked at my mother. She had tears in her eyes. That quick glimpse at those we loved tore at our hearts.

One morning, after we had just woken up, my mother announced, "Listen, everybody, today our journey is coming to an end. I had a strange dream. I was walking toward a clay hut with a flat roof and no windows. As I tried to enter I hit my head because the doorway was so low. It was dark inside, but I could see a woman dressed in white in the middle of the room. Her back was toward me, and I could tell she was mixing something in a huge kettle on the stove."

I could see some of the people in the wagon were laughing at her. I didn't like anybody to laugh at my mother. I knew she was psychic and often saw things before they happened.

A few hours later the train stopped. No station name was announced, but we could hear loud Russian voices outside. The door opened, and a soldier shouted, "*Vykhodite!* Come out!"

We gathered our belongings and climbed onto trucks that were waiting outside the train. We saw Ciocia Stefa, Zosia, and Nina being pushed onto another truck. "Let us be together with my sister," I heard Ciocia Stefa plead, pointing at us. The soldiers ignored her. We were in the middle of nowhere—there was no station; there were no trees. There was just flat land all around us. The trucks started up. The truck holding Ciocia Stefa and my cousins went in the opposite direction. We waved to them and cried. They threw kisses at us and disappeared into the distance.

We traveled for hours on a dusty road across a tawny steppe that stretched to the horizon. No vehicles passed us. There was no sign of human life. There was only vast loneliness and solitude.

At last we reached a village of flat-roofed dwellings with no windows. They reminded me of pictures of Arab clay huts in the desert that I had once seen in a magazine. Strange-looking people, olive-skinned, with flat faces and high cheekbones, met my eyes. The men wore round gray hats, and their beards were split in two in the center. The older women wore loose-fitting white garments and scarves wound around their heads in elaborate patterns. The younger women and the girls had uncovered heads; their hair hung in long plaits down their backs. Their long-sleeved dresses were different colors—mostly gray, mauve, and yellow—and were tied with narrow belts.

The crowd, chattering in a strange language, surrounded the trucks. One of the men stretched his hands out toward me. I screamed and pulled back. My mother, who was behind me, said, "Don't be afraid. He wants to help you down." I let him take me down from the truck. We sat on our suitcases in the middle of the square, and the unfamiliar-looking people stared at us. The children, braver, came up and touched our clothing. The people seemed friendly but surprised to see us. I wondered who they could be.

The trucks left. We had no idea what would happen next. A man with an air of authority about him came out of one of the huts and spoke to the crowd. Of course, we didn't understand anything he said.

In the distance, against the blue sky, I saw a huge animal with two humps. "It's a camel," my mother explained. A young woman with long black hair in two braids was milking the camel. When she finished, she came toward us with a bucket and a mug. She dipped the mug into the bucket and handed it to me. It smelled like rotten vegetables, and when I drank it, it tasted very sour. I didn't like it, but I was hungry, so I drank some.

The woman went around distributing the camel's milk to everybody.

Finally, the man who had spoken to the crowd before, whom the people called Commissar, motioned us toward one of the huts. Lala, Babcia, Janek, and Pani Irena and her two daughters followed. I was happy to see that Graźyna and Marysia, with their mothers and sisters, were ordered to come with us, too.

Inside the hut it was dark and smelled like cow manure. Wooden bunks lined the walls. We put our suitcases on the bunks and stared around us in despair.

"Stay here with your brother," my mother said. "I am going to buy some food."

I couldn't imagine where she would find any food or, if she did, how she would manage to buy some in this

I had never seen a camel, nor drunk camel's milk, until we arrived in Central Asia. © *Ralko/Dreamstime.com*

strange language. But when she came back she carried a small clay container of milk (cow's milk, thankfully) and a thin, round, flat bread that looked like a large pancake. The bread was dry, but to me it tasted like the best cake I had ever eaten. I savored every bite.

Then I noticed a bump on my mother's forehead. "What happened, Mamusiu?" I asked, pointing at the bump.

"I walked into a low doorway and hit my head," she told me. "A woman in a white dress was stirring milk. I traded my woolen scarf for some milk and a piece of bread. It was the same house that was in my dream."

I wished that the people on the train who had laughed at her this morning were here now to hear her story and see the bump on her forehead.

The night was very cold. We huddled together on one of the bunks for warmth. I covered my face with a blanket, but by morning my whole body felt like a piece of ice.

"Keep moving, keep moving," my mother advised. "I will go to see what we can do next."

She went out, and when she came back she said, "Pack up. We're moving. I managed to get a room in a house. The man spoke Russian and agreed to take us in. I gave him some money, but I don't know how long we can stay.

"There are no guards," she continued, "and the commissar is nowhere to be seen, so we have to take this risk. We have to leave this freezing place." Just as she had found food for us in this strange land yesterday, today she found us a better place to live. Lala, Janek, and Babcia wanted to come with us, and my mother agreed that they could.

Collecting our few belongings, we walked toward a rectangular mud house. We entered it through a long, dark corridor, which led to a large room. In the middle was a huge iron pot built into the brick stove. It was full of milk. I could see a fire burning under the pot, its flames lighting a small area of the room. A young man appeared with an oil lamp in his hand and motioned us through another dark tunnel into a small room with a linen curtain instead of a door. The house smelled of sour milk, and the air was stale and stuffy, but it was warm. We had some blankets, which we put on the clay floor.

The man reappeared, pulling open the curtain and smiling, and gestured us to follow him. He led us to a spacious room with colorful quilts hanging on the walls and soft covers on the floor. In the middle of the room was a low, round table surrounded by small cushions. An older man stood up and bowed to us. Three boys, all under the age of 10, were running around the room. An old woman sat in the corner.

The young man spoke to us in Russian: "Sit down, please." We squatted around the table. A young woman carrying a tray joined us. She placed the tray, which held hard-boiled eggs, more of the flat bread I had eaten the day before, and a jug of milk, in front of the old man. The old woman passed out colorful wooden bowls to everybody, and the young woman poured the milk into them. The old man peeled the eggs and cut them in half, broke the bread into small pieces with his hands, and passed the food around on the tray. We each took half an egg and a piece of bread and drank the milk, cupping our hands around the bowls. The women smiled at us in a friendly manner.

I had a strange feeling that none of this was real, that it was a dream or something out of the Aladdin tales from the books I loved to read. I closed my eyes for a moment, but when I opened them I was still there in a strange land with unfamiliar people. Hunger made me realize how grateful I was for this meal.

My mother broke the silence by asking the young man in her broken Russian, "What is this place called?"

He replied, "You are in Akdendek, Kazakhstan." His words meant nothing to me.

The old man cut into the conversation in his own language. Apparently the young man was the only one who could speak Russian. He said, "He is my father." Then he translated for the old man: "My grandfather had a lot of land and many goats. He was rich but now everything is gone." Then the two men put their fingers over their mouths and looked around in fear. With what we had just gone through, I knew why they were afraid.

The feast ended, and we thanked our hosts, bowing to them, and went back to our room.

That night, a scream woke me up. Babcia cried, "Look! Look at the walls!" I gazed at them in horror; they were covered with crawling cockroaches.

"Let's leave! Let's leave!" shouted Lala.

"We can't leave in the middle of the night and wake up those kind people," my mother replied.

Luckily Antek and Janek did not wake up. I didn't sleep for the rest of the night. By the light of the dim oil lamp, I watched, petrified, as hundreds of shiny brown cockroaches scurried across the walls. I shook them off me and brushed them off my sleeping brother when some of them fell onto him from the ceiling. In the morning we gathered our belongings, shook out all the cockroaches, and left. We moved back into the cold hut.

7

Traveling by Oxcart

We lived in the freezing dwelling for a week. Then one morning we were awakened by a loud knock on the door.

"Open up!" The commissar was standing there with a notebook in his hand. He called out the names of three families, and one of them was ours. The other two were Lala's and Pani Irena's.

"Pack up," he instructed. "You're leaving."

Three carts, the kind that transport vegetables to the market, each pulled by an ox, were waiting for us outside.

"Why us, why us? Where are you taking us?" Babcia cried.

"We are going to be shot!" wailed Pani Irena.

"Don't say that in front of the children!" my mother scolded.

But it was too late. I had heard her, and I was afraid.

We climbed into the carts. There was one for each family plus a Kazakh driver wearing a short gray quilted coat and a round fur hat. We were political prisoners, but we didn't need any guards, because we were just women and young children. Where could we go if we escaped? Into the vast, empty steppes?

Marysia and Grażyna rushed out of the dwelling toward our cart. I could see tears running down their cheeks. I tried hard not to cry myself. It was all I could do to call, "*Żegnajcie*! Good-bye!" I wondered if we would ever see each other again. They stood in front of the open door, waving, as we drove away in the carts. Eventually they disappeared in the distance and our slow journey into the unknown began.

It was late April, and the spring air was clear but very crisp; patches of white snow were still scattered across the land. Purple and yellow flowers covered the steppes like a carpet. A few low bushes of grayish green dotted the empty fields.

Lala, Babcia, and Janek were in the first cart, my mother and Antek and I were in the middle one, and Pani Irena and her daughters were behind us. After many hours of traveling, we suddenly heard the driver of the cart behind us shout. We looked back and saw his ox sitting in the middle of the road. The driver screamed, "*Hula, hula!*" and hit the ox with a whip. Antek started to cry; he couldn't stand seeing somebody being cruel to animals. The ox didn't move. The other drivers decided to wait for it. They let us get out and stretch our legs while they smoked their pipes and chattered in their language. After about an hour the ox stood up and we moved on.

The sun, a huge orange ball, was sinking into the horizon. Night was coming. The sound of water reached our ears, and soon we came upon a small stream. The carts stopped. The drivers untied the oxen and let them graze. They gathered a few stones, cut some branches from a small bush, and made a fire. Producing an iron

An early spring landscape like this one surrounded us as we continued our journey by oxcart. © *Maxim Petrichuk/Dreamstime.com*

kettle, they boiled some water, into which they dropped tea leaves. We each had a mug, and the drivers offered us the tea, which they called hot chai, and some pieces of dry meat. We slept in the carts with the moon shining on us.

"Hula, hula." The voices woke me up. The carts were moving again. The steppes gave way to small grassy hills with low bushes. Goats, followed by Kazakh shepherds, appeared. The drivers and shepherds exchanged greetings: *"Salem, salem."*

After a few more hours of travel, we heard sounds of knocking and grinding in the near distance. Soon we passed some houses made of clay, all identical, with sloping roofs and small windows. We stopped at a long, rectangular building. The smell of roasting meat and freshly baked bread filled the air. Men in yellow helmets and muddy gray clothes marched into the building; their tired faces hardly glanced in our direction. Our drivers left, too, to enter the building.

"Wait here, everybody," my mother said. "I will go see if we can buy some food." Pani Irena went with her, but they soon returned empty-handed.

"We are near a gold mine," my mother explained. "The cafeteria is for miners and people who have work permits. They wouldn't sell us anything."

We sat in the carts, disappointed and hungry. A middle-aged Russian woman came around the corner of the building, wearing the gray quilted coat I had seen on most of the people. She was holding something tightly under her coat, and as she approached our carts, she looked furtively around. Seeing nobody but us, she pulled some loaves of bread out from under her coat and threw one into each of our carts. "*Dieti, dieti.* Children, children," she exclaimed.

As she turned to leave, my mother called out "*Spasibo, spasibo!* Thank you, thank you!" Then my mother took out a knife and cut three slices from the round, golden-crusted loaf. "We have to leave some for later," she said. "We don't know when we will next have any food."

As I ate slowly, enjoying the warm bread, I remembered one day in Poland when I gave some of my money to a beggar woman sitting on the step of the church. I had felt very sorry for her. Now were we the homeless beggars arousing pity in others? The gnawing hunger that the bread barely satisfied stifled any other feelings I might have had; I was only grateful to our angel of mercy.

At nightfall we reached our final destination. After passing through a Kazakh village with the usual flat roofs and walled huts, we came to a row of square huts with windows. At the end of the street the carts stopped in front of a long building. A stout, young, blond Russian woman in that same gray coat, with a long black skirt and brown boots underneath, ordered us to unload the carts.

"*Zdravstvuyte,*" she barked. "Greetings. I am Natasha, and I am in charge here. You are in Akbuzal. You are not allowed to go out of the village further than one kilometer or you will be arrested."

We were already arrested, I thought.

"The workers' meetings are held every week in the main building by my office. Long live *Sovietskiy Soyuz* and our glorious motherland." She turned and marched briskly and decisively away.

Let *Sovietskiy Soyuz* die and to hell with the motherland, I silently wished. I tried to suppress these bad thoughts, but could not. The happy, trusting child I had been was gone. I was acquiring adult language, and, unfortunately, I was learning to hate.

PART III

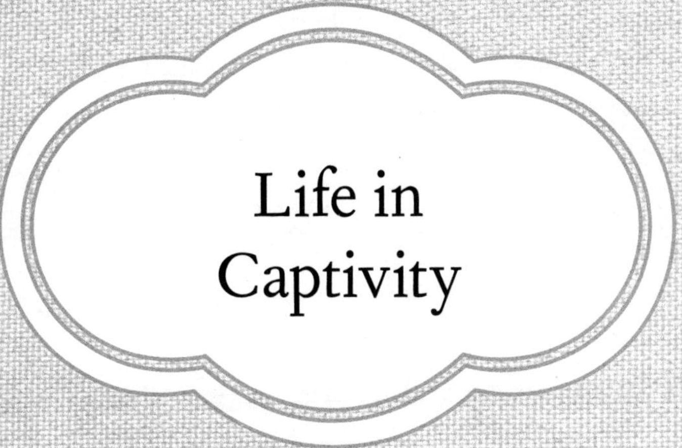

Life in Captivity

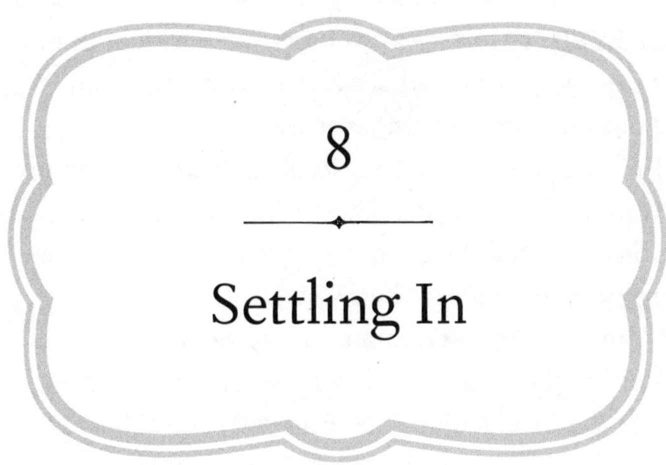

8

Settling In

The door of the long, rectangular building opened, and a Russian man, also wearing a gray coat and a round fur hat, came out. "*Zdravstvuyte*," he greeted us in a loud voice. "I am Ivan, assistant to Natasha, who is in charge of this *kolkhoz*, communal farm. Get out of your carts and bring your belongings with you."

We did as he ordered. My mother, Antek, and I, along with Lala, Babcia, Janek, Pani Irena, Danusia, and Ewa, followed him into a long, dark shack. Rows of wooden bunks ran along two sides of the walls, facing each other, supported by wooden legs that were sunken into the clay floor. In the center, two heavy, long tables stretched from one end of the room to the other. On the wall opposite the doorway was a small window, the only source of light. A smoky wood-burning stove stood in one corner. I didn't see any chairs. We picked our bunks, and my mother spread a blanket over the rough wood and put our suitcases underneath.

Before we had time to settle down, another group arrived, also via oxcart. They joined our group of three families. A middle-aged, heavily built woman and a young girl introduced themselves.

"I am Kulakowska, and this is my daughter Litka."

Behind them came an elderly woman with short gray hair and a kind smile, accompanied by a tall, slim, and pretty young woman with large blue eyes, who carried two suitcases.

"Dzień dobry," they greeted us. "I am Rzewuska, and this is my daughter Lila," said the older woman. "My daughter is a ballet teacher."

I was interested only in Litka, a blonde girl a little taller than me, who wore a friendly expression. I needed a companion. We exchanged glances and were immediately drawn to each other. I walked over to her and introduced myself.

"I am Krysia, and I know that you are Litka. I'm almost 10."

"I'm 14," she answered. "Let's go outside."

We walked onto a dirt road lined with square mud huts with small windows and slanting roofs. There were no people outside. Where was everybody? I wondered. One of the buildings bore a sign reading *Kantoor* (office). The door to the next building was open, and we went in.

It looked like a store, but the shelves were empty except for tubes of toothpaste and pink bottles of perfume. A stout, gray-haired man stared at us from behind the counter.

"Why do they sell toothpaste if there is nothing to eat?" Litka exclaimed. The man didn't understand her and just sat there in silence, a bored look on his face.

Walking back toward our shack, we noticed two long buildings in the distance, on a hill. The strong smell of cow manure drifting in the air made me think they must be barns. We were surrounded by small treeless hills; very low bushes grew here and there. In the fields stretching around the buildings, we saw people working: bending, carrying heavy bags, and stacking them into piles. We were too far away to see what they were gathering into the bags.

The next day Ivan and Natasha came to our shack together. "We are taking you to do farmwork," Natasha commanded in her unpleasant, shrill voice. "Only elderly people and children do not work. Afterward, the workers' meeting will be held in the office." Babcia, Pani Rzewuska, Litka, Danusia, and Ewa stayed in the shack with Janek, Antek, and me. My mother walked out the door with the other adults, but soon returned.

"I have permission to see a doctor in the town of Georgiewka, and I have to leave as soon as possible. Look after your brother," she said to me. The next day a hired cart pulled by an ox took her away. Four days passed before she came back with permission not to work. I didn't understand why, and she didn't offer any explanations.

During the days that my mother was gone, Litka and I were very curious to hear what was said at the workers' meetings. We were not allowed into the office, but we sneaked behind the building, where we could hear Natasha's voice very clearly.

"You Polish *svoloch*—animals—you fed on the blood and sweat of the underprivileged for too long. Your time of punishment has come. Work hard for the glory of our country. In time you will become Communists." My Russian was not very good, so I couldn't understand everything, but I did understand the insults, and was shocked. I looked at Litka and saw how outraged she was, too. We walked away before anybody could come out of the meeting and see us.

When Lala, the pianist, came back from the meeting, she cried bitterly and complained to her mother, Babcia. "What is going to happen to my hands? They will be ruined by the hard labor in the fields. I will never be able to play the piano again." I felt very sorry for her as I watched Babcia, tears in her eyes, embrace and try to console her daughter.

We were issued coupons for food, which was in short supply. On some days a line formed in front of the store where bread, rationed to one slice per person, could be obtained. I would wait in the line with my mother, watching the government shopkeeper cut thick slices of dark bread that had the consistency of a wet rubber sponge. Extra water had been added to the dough to make it heavier, but it also made the bread soggy, sticky, and chewy. Each slice was dense and tasteless, but anything edible meant the difference between life and starvation.

The worst days were when we waited in vain; those days, when we got close to the counter, the last piece of bread would be given to somebody in front of us and the shopkeeper would proclaim the two dreaded words "*Ne khvataet*. There is none left."

The communal farm had milk from the cows and potatoes and sometimes tomatoes and corn from the fields, but everything was reserved for the NKVD police and the Soviet army. The workers could buy potatoes that were the size of plums and considered not good enough for the army. The consequences of stealing could be harsh—the usual punishment was to be sent to a concentration camp, where you were always surrounded by guards—but everybody did it anyway. Everybody who worked in the fields, that is. Since my mother didn't work, she resorted to bartering. She had sewn golden coins and jewelry into her clothing, exchanging the gold for stolen food and opium—a sedative and narcotic drug made from poppy seeds—which my mother would trade to the Kazakhs for food. The opium slabs looked like chocolate bars wrapped in brown paper. The Kazakhs loved to smoke the opium in long pipes.

An old Kazakh, Kuran, used to bring my mother the opium, but he was very secretive about it. Usually they would meet behind the shack, away from prying eyes. I was not allowed to listen to his and my mother's conversations.

I was very curious about Kuran and the exchanges between him and my mother. One day I asked her, "How does he get those brown slabs? Who gives them to him?"

She replied, "The mine sells an allotted quantity to mine workers in the town that we passed on our way here. Kuran buys them from them and then comes here to exchange it for gold and clothing. The Kazakhs who need more opium and have no way of getting it bargain with me for milk or sometimes a piece of meat or freshly baked flat bread. This is the only way that I can get food for us since I'm not working in the fields. It's not legal," she warned me, "so remember never to say anything to anybody about it! We have to survive the best way we can manage."

Even though I was not allowed to be present during my mother's bargaining, I learned how to barter myself.

I made friends with a Kazakh girl named Ashana, who was about my age. Her thick, dark, braided hair hung down to her waist, and whenever we met she always wore a broad smile. Sometimes she would invite me to her home. She showed me the dolls that her mother had sewn for her from scraps of colorful material and stuffed with something that might have been beans. I couldn't ask what it was because I knew only a few words of the Kazakhs' language. Somehow we managed to communicate with sign language and a few Russian words.

Ashana was also my source of information. My mother would give me a blouse, a scarf, or a pair of gloves to barter for eggs or milk—mostly for eggs—and Ashana knew where I could get them.

The Kazakh village was near the Russian houses where we lived. The flat-roofed mud houses were windowless, with long, dark corridors. One day, as I entered the total darkness of one of the huts, I heard a dog barking. I froze. Then a female voice shouted at the dog and a woman appeared, carrying an oil lamp. In the dim light I saw her holding a large black dog by the neck. It was still snarling at me.

"*Salem, jumurdka bar?*" I greeted her, asking if she had any eggs. She nodded. She pushed the dog into a room and locked it in, then motioned me into another chamber and looked at the pink blouse I was carrying. She showed me six of her fingers—six eggs.

"*Nyet, nyet,*" I protested. I counted to 12 using my fingers.

She shook her head. She displayed nine fingers.

"*Da, da,*" I nodded. I was very proud of myself as I walked home.

But when I told my mother the story of how I obtained the eggs, she scolded me. "I forbid you to walk alone into the dark corridors again. Next time I will come with you."

I knew that, being a child, I could get more than she could, because the Kazakhs were kind people who liked children. But I was also afraid of dogs.

9

Strange Happenings at Night

When we had first arrived in Akbuzal, each family had been allowed to write one letter to Poland. My mother wrote to her oldest sister, Hala. Every day Antek and Janek watched for trucks arriving at the office in hopes that one of them would carry mail for us.

After several weeks of waiting, I heard a knock. Lila jumped from her bunk and rushed to open the door of our shack. Ivan announced, "Here are some letters for you."

"*Spasibo,*" Lila thanked him as she grabbed the correspondence.

"Pani Zosia," she called to my mother, "this is for you. And this one is for Pani Kulakowska. Nothing for me."

Her hands shaking, my mother opened the envelope Lila had handed her.

Dear Pani Zosia,

I am well and thinking of you. I am sending you two parcels. Hoping you will receive them. Stefa, Nina, and Zosia are in a village near you and are doing well.

Everything else above the signature was censored in black ink. The letter was signed "Mila."

My mother's voice was choked with emotion. "This is your father's writing. I recognize it. He couldn't sign his name, but he is trying to let us know that he is alive. Thank God for that."

I was so happy to hear her words. I missed my father very much and prayed every night for his safety.

A week after we received my father's letter, a knock on the door awoke me in the middle of the night. I heard Ivan's voice shouting, "*Tovarisch* Mihulka, come to the *kantoor*!" The Russians always addressed the adults as *tovarisch* rather than the friendlier *comrade*.

My mother quickly dressed and left. I couldn't sleep anymore. I began shaking with fear. What did they want from her? What if they arrest her and put her in jail and I never see her again? What will happen to Antek and me?

I heard other people moving in their bunks. Ivan's knock and shout had awakened them, too, but nobody came to console me. I was alone, with Antek sleeping peacefully next to me.

Time dragged on. I didn't know how many hours were passing, but the night seemed very long. Even if I had had a watch, it was too dark to see anything. The one small oil lamp that we had on the table was turned off.

I tried to think of happy times in Poland: our vacations in the Karpaty (Carpathian) Mountains, swimming in the clear water of flowing rivers, hiking, and stopping for a picnic under the shade of pine trees. But my thoughts kept returning to my mother. What were they doing to her?

Tocha, my mother's youngest sister, played with me during one summer vacation in the Karpaty Mountains, one of our family's favorite places.

I wanted to jump out of bed and run to the office to save her, but I knew that I was helpless against the people who held her. And maybe I was afraid to face the fact that she might be gone; maybe I wanted to hold on a little longer to the hope that she would come back. Finally, the door opened, and there was my mother, pale and tired but smiling at me. She embraced me and held me close while I cried with joy at having her back.

"What did the NKVD want from you?" I asked.

"Everything is fine. Don't worry. They just asked me a few questions about your father."

A few questions took all night? I thought. But I knew that she would not tell me anything more.

After my mother thought I had fallen back asleep, I heard her talking to Pani Rzewuska and Babcia. "The NKVD directed lamps at my face and repeated the same questions about my husband over and over, trying to wear me out. They wanted me to sign a confession that my husband had been a judge before the war, but I refused. I told them he was an accountant, because for some reason the Communists consider that to be a nonthreatening occupation. I also said that I did not know where he was—which is the truth. I was so afraid that they would take me away and I would never see my children again. The Soviets invaded my country, seized my home, all my possessions, and deprived me of my freedom—what else do they want from me?" she cried.

Hearing the emotion in my mother's voice made my heart ache for her and what she had been through. But at the same time, I was so relieved to have her back after all those hours of waiting that I was finally able to relax and fall asleep.

After that night, every time we saw a truck by the office we knew that the NKVD had arrived at the kolkhoz. Antek and Janek were usually the ones to run to our shack, shouting, "They're here!"

Sometimes the NKVD would leave during the day, but on other occasions they would stay into the night, and my mother, or somebody else in our group, would be awakened from her sleep and called to the office for interrogation. Every time this happened I went through the same agony of waiting, praying, and fearing the worst.

Doesn't the NKVD ever sleep? Why do they do everything at night? I asked myself during those tormented hours. They arrested us in the middle of the night, and now they won't leave my mother alone. Are they so ashamed of what they are doing that they are trying to cover up their deeds in the dark? All I knew was they were mean and cruel and I hated them. I had been taught to forgive our enemies, but I could not find it in my heart to forgive the NKVD.

September, the beginning of fall, brought relief from the unbearable heat of the summer days and the swarms of mosquitoes. There was never enough to eat, and we had all lost weight and grown skinny—except for my mother, who was getting fatter. I wondered how that was possible.

One day Ivan came to our shack and ordered my mother and Pani Rzewuska to lift the heavy tables that stood in the middle of it. One was needed for the office, and since everybody else was working in the fields, my mother and Pani Rzewuska were the only ones who could do it. That evening my mother said she wasn't feeling very well.

In our shack, sheets and blankets hung from the ceiling to the bottoms of the bunks, forming partitions between each family to create a sense of some privacy. I saw my mother whisper something to Pani Irena, whose bunk was at the very end of the shack. Pani Irena came to me and said, "Get your nightgown. Tonight you and Antek will sleep next to my daughters." I thought this was a very strange request, but it didn't occur to me to question her. I was used to obeying adults. I had learned a long time ago that there was always a reason for what they said, but often nobody bothered to explain anything to children.

Antek and I fell asleep immediately. In the middle of the night I woke to the sound of moaning and crying. Listening attentively, I recognized my mother's voice. I was just about to jump out of bed when Pani Rzewuska appeared by my side and whispered, "Do not go anywhere near your mother; she is very sick. Pray for her very hard—let's pray together. Our Father who art in heaven . . ." Were there tears in her eyes, or was it my imagination?

I peeked out from behind the curtain and saw the veterinarian sitting on the opposite bunk. I knew who he was because I had seen him tending to the cows in the barn. But what was he doing here?

"Go back to sleep now," Pani Rzewuska said.

But I couldn't sleep. My body was shaking with fear. I wanted to help my mother, to stop her pain. I looked out, past the curtain, again, and as my eyes adjusted to the dim light shed by the one oil lamp sitting on the table, I noticed Pani Rzewuska and Pani Irena moving silently, carrying towels and a bucket of water.

Eventually I fell asleep. I dreamed that a baby was crying. Was it a dream?

When I woke up again the early light was pouring into the shack through the only window, illuminating the rows of hanging blankets. My first thought was to see my mother. I jumped out of the bunk and ran to our space.

My mother was in bed, looking very pale. She smiled, embraced me, and held me very close. Why was she so especially happy to see me? I wondered. But I didn't ask any questions.

A few days after that strange night I was with my friend Ashana. By now I had learned a few more Russian and Kazakh words and could understand her better. She said, "I heard that a baby was born to somebody. Do you know anything about this?"

"No, I don't," I replied.

But I knew that everybody was hiding something from me. I could tell by the whispers and glances that began whenever I walked into the shack.

I went to my mother. "I know from Ashana that a baby was born here. Tell me the truth."

My mother took my hand, and we walked out into the hills. The weather was getting colder, and dark clouds were gathering in the sky. There was a feeling of foreboding in the air.

My mother pointed to a pile of stones covering a hole at the bottom of one of the hills. "You had a baby sister," she said. "She was born too soon." Without a doctor, hospital, or incubator, she explained, the baby had died.

I was stunned by her words. Then I felt anger beginning to build, overcoming me. "Why did you let her die?" I screamed. "Why didn't you let me see her? I always wanted a sister! How could you do this to me?" Although my words were directed at my mother, part of me knew that I wasn't really upset with her; I was expressing my fury at our fate and blaming the Soviets who had put us in this horrible situation.

"It is better that this happened," my mother answered in a resigned tone. "The baby would have died sooner or later from malnutrition or disease. She had no chance of survival in the conditions we are living in now.

"Pani Rzewuska baptized her and named her Barbara," she continued. "She and the old Kazakh Kuran put her into a shoebox and buried her here, behind those rocks."

My mother looked so sad that the anger left me. In its place was sorrow—for her as well as for me. Tears rushed down my cheeks; I cried and cried, mourning my sister.

"Be happy that I am alive and able to take care of you," my mother said. "I didn't want you to be hurt."

"What about Tatuś?" I asked. "He will be very sad when he hears about this."

My mother replied, "Yes, he will be sad, but he will understand."

She embraced me, and we slowly walked back together in silence.

I didn't know where babies came from, and didn't know that my mother had nearly died during the delivery.

10

Enduring the Winter

Winter was coming, and with it the fear of being left without fuel during the harsh weather ahead. During the summer Litka, Janek, my brother Antek, and I had gathered dry cow and sheep manure that covered the pastures surrounding the kolkhoz. It burned well, with no bad smells. It couldn't be stored, because it soon disintegrated into sand, so the workers on the kolkhoz had a special method for hardening it. They mixed the fresh manure with straw, formed it into bricks in special wooden containers that had been made for that purpose, dried it in the sun, watered it, and then dried it again. After they repeated this process several times, the mixture hardened and was ready to be distributed to NKVD officials and barn managers.

One day Litka said to me, "We can do that ourselves."

"What, gather fresh manure and mix it with our hands?" I exclaimed.

"So what? Do you want to freeze in the winter?"

"No, I don't. We'll have to do it."

The next day Litka's mother, Pani Kulakowska, managed to get tin buckets for us. Litka and I followed the cows and goats that were grazing on the hills. Some of the shepherds were not too happy to see us and chased us away, but most of them allowed us to gather the fresh manure. The only way to pick it up was to use pieces of plywood that we found around one of the barns. Then we had to carry our full buckets to a sunny, flat, and dry surface next to the wall of our shack and spread the manure on the ground. We added straw to it and formed rounds that looked like huge pancakes. We let them dry, sprayed them with water, and then let them dry again. Antek and Janek wanted to help, but we considered them too young and allowed them only to gather straw and carry water. Except for the stench, it was like making mud pies in the sand. Since we had no toys or books and didn't go to school, this was a good way of entertaining ourselves.

One day Natasha, the NKVD official who was in charge of the kolkhoz, walked by as we were working. She stopped and praised us. "Great job. Your *kiziaki* look good. I can see that you are hard workers. Next year you will be allowed to sort potatoes to benefit the kolkhoz."

"Is that going to be our future?" whispered Litka.

"Be quiet. She might hear us," I warned.

"She doesn't understand Polish. And I hate her," Litka retorted angrily.

"So do I, but we have to be careful about what we say." I wanted to cry but knew that I couldn't change our situation. We had to finish before dark, so, with a heavy heart, I continued to work.

When we were satisfied that the *kiziaki* were hard enough, we carried them inside the shack and stored them behind the stove, in the space provided for that purpose. Babcia, Janek's grandmother, watched us and said, "You should be proud of what you have done. Let's hope there will be enough fuel to last until spring."

By early November the weather was getting colder and colder. Food was scarce, and I was always hungry. I got sick and had to stay in bed. My mother was sure that I had a kidney problem and fed me unsalted hot water with buckwheat swimming in it, which she called soup. This was the only treatment she could give me.

Luckily a parcel arrived from my aunt in Poland. It was one of the few that were not stolen, and it contained rice, sugar, and chocolate, as well as a drawing pad and box of crayons for me and a little red car for Antek. We were thrilled, even though my mother said, "We will have to ration what we received so that it will last longer."

Our joy was short lived. That same afternoon somebody knocked on the door. Lila opened it. Two unfamiliar NKVD, wearing their dark-green uniforms, entered and nodded slightly in greeting. I was surprised to see them because usually they came at night and ordered people to the office. Ivan and Natasha were not with them.

"*Zdravstuyte*, we have come to take your children away to the *dietkommune*." One of the men looked at the list and read, "Two children from the Mihulka family and one from Lala Dombrowska's." That meant me, Antek, and Janek.

I pulled the bedcovers over my head. My body shivered and my teeth started to chatter. I understood that he was going to take us to an orphanage. Trying to stay invisible, I peeked out from under the blanket without drawing attention to myself. My brother had grabbed my mother tightly and was holding onto her, burrowing his head into her neck. Janek was on his grandmother's lap, not quite understanding what was going on. His mother, Lala, was sobbing loudly.

My mother screamed in her broken Russian, "You are not going to take my children away! Over my dead body! You took my country, my home, destroyed my life, and now you think that you can take my children away?"

One of the NKVD said, "This is for the good of the children. We will give them food and an excellent education, and we will bring them up as loyal Communists for the glory of the Soviet Union."

My mother shrieked back, "My daughter is sick. You cannot take a sick child in this weather. I will never let you take my children away. Do you have any children? How would you like your children to be taken away from you?"

The taller, older NKVD, who seemed to be the senior one, whispered something to the other man. The man walked outside.

My heart was pounding. What would be next? Would they use force to take us away?

Then the unexpected happened. The remaining NKVD took off his hat, put it over his heart, and replied, "Yes, I have two children, but I have to obey my orders. I will not take your children away today, but in three days I will be back. By that time your daughter will get better and be able to travel. *Do svidania.* Goodbye." He turned around, put his hat back on his head, and walked out.

The next three days were the longest of my life. I could not imagine going to a Russian orphanage. I prayed for a miracle. "Please, God, help us. Don't take us away from our mother. Have mercy on us and send us a miracle."

The third day came, and by the afternoon there was still no NKVD car in sight.

"They like to come at night," Babcia reminded us.

"You are a pessimist; you do not believe in miracles," retorted my mother.

But a miracle did happen. The snow came down and covered the ground so high that no car or oxcart could travel in it. The NKVD would not be able to get through. I started to breathe more easily, and my health started to improve.

I often wondered why the door to our shack opened toward the inside, and not out, and why a long ladder was kept indoors near the door. When winter came, I found out. When the snow fell, it was so high that it nearly reached the top of the roof. The only way to get out was to open the door and shovel the soft snow into buckets. (We needed the melted snow for drinking and washing, as we had no running water.) When enough snow had been cleared away for the ladder to be taken outside, it was propped against the snow that had already hardened, forming a wall. If we needed to get out of the shack, we would climb up the ladder. On days when it was not snowing, buckets full of snow could be taken up the ladder and thrown out. Sometimes axes had to be used instead of shovels.

One day, as it was getting toward evening, Babcia asked me to come with her to get some milk at the barn. "Now is the milking time," she said, "and if we are lucky, they will sell it to us. I would like you to come with me."

"*Dobrze.* Okay," I replied.

I put on a warm coat, gloves, and my long boots called *pimy*, which were made of sheepskin and did not let the cold penetrate, and tied a woolen scarf around my head. Ordinary shoes and boots were not suitable for the Russian climate, so my mother had bought us *pimy*. Some people called them *valenki*.

My mother was busy at the stove at the other end of the shack, so I didn't tell her I was leaving. It hadn't snowed for several days, so somebody had left the ladder

In the harsh Kazakhstan winter, we wore boots like these, which some people called *pimy* and others called *valenki*.
© Kokhanchikov/Shutterstock.com

outside. Babcia and I climbed up and headed toward the barn. The ground was crusted over, and we had no trouble walking on the firmly packed snow.

The milking was in progress, and we had to wait a long time. The supervisor, a short, muscular woman, came around and asked us, "Do you have a permit to buy the milk?"

Babcia's Russian was very bad. She said, "*Ne ponimayu*. I don't understand."

I couldn't help her, because I didn't know anything about permits. The supervisor waved her hand in dismissal and walked away.

Disappointed, we walked outside into the freezing-cold night. Snow started falling so heavily that we couldn't see any chimneys of the buildings below. Babcia started walking in the opposite direction from our shack. I knew she was wrong. "*Nie, nie,*" I insisted, "this is not the right way to go." Babcia kept pulling me, and I resisted.

Suddenly we saw glowing lights moving toward us in the darkness. The village was covered in snow up to the rooftops, so they could not have been coming from any windows. I didn't know what the lights were, but I knew that we had to find our way home as quickly as possible. Please, God, guide us, I prayed silently.

Babcia was slowing down, puffing and panting with exhaustion. More and more lights glistened in the dark. What were they?

In the distance a wisp of smoke drifted out of the flat, snow-covered ground.

"Look, Babcia, maybe it's our shack. *Szybko, szybko!* Hurry, hurry!" I pulled her with all the strength I could muster, until we reached the smoky area.

Luckily the end of the ladder was still visible. The steps were covered with snow, so I started sliding down, but only far enough to bang on the door. My mother opened it, but first she had to get a shovel to push the snow aside to get me. Babcia was still at the top waiting to be rescued by Lala and Pani Irena.

My mother threw her arms around me and cried, "Where have you been?"

"We went to buy some milk. We could see lots of lights, so it wasn't completely dark."

"Lots of lights? Lots of lights? What do you mean?"

"Lights that were moving toward us."

"They were wolves!" My mother cried out. "The lights were their eyes. You could have been eaten! Oh my God! Why did you leave without my permission?"

"I'm sorry, Mamusiu. We were only going to be gone a short time, but then we had to wait at the barn."

My mother turned toward Babcia and yelled at her. "How could you take my child and not tell me? Don't you know there are hungry wolves looking for food?"

Babcia's voice shook with emotion. "I'm sorry. I didn't realize how dangerous it was to walk outside."

I was shocked—and glad that I hadn't known about the wolves, because I would have been even more terrified.

It was Christmas 1940, and we had no tree. The only food we had left was buckwheat and dry bread. On Christmas Eve my mother, Lila, and Pani Irena spread a white sheet on the one table that stood in the middle of the shack. Pani Rzewuska found some candles and lit them. Pani Kulakowska cooked the buckwheat soup and ladled it into tin bowls.

We all gathered around the table, and Babcia started to pray. "Thank you, God, for all the gifts that we are about to receive. Please help us in our hour of need and let us be free again." She choked on the last few words, and tears rolled down her cheeks.

Pieces of dry bread were on a plate instead of the usual wafer—*opłatek*—with which Polish people traditionally exchanged greetings on Christmas Eve. Everybody took a small slice and followed the beloved custom.

"*Na zdrowie*. To our health," toasted Babcia.

"May we survive this winter," added Pani Rzewuska.

"Next year we will be free," pronounced my mother. "America and England will save us."

Everybody looked at her. "You are always such an optimist," remarked Babcia.

"Hope is the only thing we have, and I have a good feeling about our future."

"As long as it makes you happy," said Lala.

Suddenly a howling wind rushed through the chimney and put out the fire in our stove, our only source of heat.

"We'll freeze!" cried Lila.

"No, we won't!" laughed my mother. "Because we are going to dance. Come on, everybody, dance!"

We formed pairs: Litka and me, Janek and Antek, my mother and Pani Rzewuska. We had to take turns because there was so little space, but we could whirl around the table.

"One, two, three polka, one, two, three polka," sang Lila, as though we were her ballet students. Those of us who weren't dancing clapped our hands until our turn came.

Once we had warmed up, we sang "Cicha noc" ("Silent Night"). The mood of the evening changed to somber, and the singing stopped. We were all lost in our own thoughts.

I went to sleep dreaming of Christmases past. Our huge tree in the living room, covered with decorations—candies in golden wrappers and round chocolate pieces covered in red foil. Most of all I remembered the Christmas Day feast of warm pierogi, roasted duck, and steaming kielbasa. On a separate table, by the window, were plates of gingerbreads, nut cakes, and rolls of poppy-seed loaves. My father, my mother's four sisters, my uncles, and my cousins were all there talking and laughing. I wanted to stay in the dream, but I woke up because somebody was shaking my arm.

My mother was sitting on the edge of the bed. She smiled and said, "*Wesołych Swiąt!* Merry Christmas! Look under your pillow. Maybe Saint Nicholas brought you something."

I lifted the pillow and grabbed something wrapped in silver foil. I unwrapped the paper, and, to my joy, a piece of chocolate met my eyes. My mother must have kept it from the time we received our last parcel from Poland. My brother had the same gift in his hand.

"*Dziękuję bardzo*, Mamusiu," I thanked my mother. I savored every bite, eating it very slowly to make it last longer.

We were buried under the snow; a storm raged above us, the wind whistled and blew violently, and wolves walked across the village in search of food. But we felt safe from the threat of the NKVD knocking on the door. At least for now!

11

Spring and Summer Surprises

In the middle of one night in early spring 1941, the familiar banging on the door of our shack woke me, and the familiar fear flooded my body. I knew the voice and the words that would follow.

"*Tovarisch* Kulakowska, *tovarisch* Kulakowska!" Natasha shouted.

I sighed with relief. It was not my mother they wanted this time; it was Litka's mother.

Somebody lit a candle, and Pani Kulakowska called out, "Coming, coming!"

The door opened, and a swish of cold night air entered. Pani Kulakowska rushed outside, and the door closed.

Even though I was glad it was not my mother who had to go to the office in the night again, I felt terribly sorry for Litka. I knew just what she would be going through for the next few hours, the agony and fear of not knowing if her mother would come back or if they would arrest her and take Litka away to an orphanage. I had spent many nights in this torment.

I wanted to go over to be with Litka and console her, but I was afraid of disturbing the others. Instead I pulled the blanket over my head and tried to shut away the world outside. I must have fallen back asleep, because the next thing I heard was the door opening and Pani Kulakowska walking in. In the early dawn light that was coming through the shack's one small, high window, I saw Litka and her mother embracing, holding each other as if they would never part. Tears were running down Pani Kulakowska's cheeks.

Then she spoke to all of us. "From now on, please do not speak about politics in front of me. I don't want to know anything about your letters from Poland."

I saw shock come over my mother's face and then knowing looks pass between the other adults in the room. I didn't understand them but knew I was not supposed to ask any questions.

That day my mother and I went for a walk. The snow was still melting after the harsh winter, but the fields were starting to bloom with early spring flowers. The air was fresh and crisp.

My mother said, "You are old enough to understand why we now have to be careful what we say in front of Litka's mother, or even Litka herself. Pani Kulakowska has joined the Communist Party and will be forced to inform on us and get evidence against anybody who speaks against the government. She told me in secret that if she had not joined, they would have taken Litka away from her and she would not have been allowed to contact her. She had to do this for Litka."

I couldn't speak. I felt sorry for Litka and her mother, but I also knew that belonging to the Communist Party meant joining the enemy camp. The Soviets had taken away our homes and imprisoned us in this terrible place. Wasn't that enough? What else did they want from us? They were torturing us emotionally, in a deceitful way that was just as harmful as physical torture.

We kept walking in silence, each of us lost in our own thoughts. I could see birds against the blue sky, returning from warmer climates where they had spent the winter. They flew from one low bush to another, looking for suitable places for their nests. I envied them. They were free. I wished I had wings and could fly back to Poland.

I must have looked very sad, because my mother said, "Let's hope that the war will be over soon. We cannot give up and dwell in despair."

"What are we going to do about Antek?" I asked. "How are we going to tell him to be careful what he says?" He was only six.

"Don't worry about him. He understands more than we know."

I knew she was right. I remembered how every time the NKVD arrived at the office, my brother and Janek would come running into the shack to warn us. If Antek was not fast enough, one of the officers would catch up and lift him up playfully. The officer would give him candy and ask him questions. Antek had learned quite a lot of Russian by playing with Russian children, but he would always reply, "*Ne znayu. Ne govoryu po-russkiy.* I don't know. I don't speak Russian." And he made sure that he took the candy, which he always shared with me.

Litka and I remained friends, but our relationship changed. I could no longer trust her and confide in her as I used to. I knew that she felt this, but we could only blame the Communists.

With the coming of spring, the snow started melting, and we had a serious problem: we couldn't let it get into the shack, where it would melt and flood us out of the only home we had. We had shovels, and Pani Kulakowska and Lila stood by the open door and tried to push the snow away, to keep it from flying inside. The task was long and tiring, and everybody had to take turns with the shovels, except for me and the younger children, who were not strong enough.

The warm weather arrived in May, and with it the empty, silent land of the steppes came alive again with vegetation. The once-bare fields were now ablaze with purple, yellow, and pink flowers, and dotted here and there with green bushes. Litka and I took long walks, enjoying the freedom of being outside after a long winter. We were taller and thinner; months of malnutrition had taken their toll on us.

The spring quickly turned into a very hot summer. Litka and I carried straw baskets and walked on sun-scorched hills, gathering *lebioda*, a green similar to spinach or chard. It grew in the wild, and when we cooked it in hot water with a little buckwheat added, we had "soup."

Often we found garlic, which looked like green onions. The cattle grazed on it, so the milk often smelled of it, and the only way to drink the milk was to pinch your nose and swallow. We were always so hungry that anything tasted good. Sometimes Antek and Janek came with us. We usually met Kazakh shepherds tending their countless flocks of sheep and goats, and they always passed us with a smile and a greeting: *"Salem, salem."*

One day we met an old man dressed in shabby gray clothes and a dirty brown hat pulled over his long gray hair. He was one of the shepherds, but when we got closer to him we saw that he looked different from the Kazakhs. He was taller, his eyes were blue, and his skin was lighter. To our surprise, he spoke to us in Polish. "*Nie bójcie się*. Don't be afraid. I am a priest in disguise. Do not tell anybody about me, but please ask your mothers if they have any Polish books I could borrow."

We promised to come back. When I told my mother about the priest, tears came to her eyes. Handing me a volume of the poems of the famous 19th-century Polish poet Adam Mickiewicz, the only book that we had brought with us from Poland, she said, "Take it to him. Let him enjoy it."

When I gave the book to the old man, his eyes lit up with happiness and gratitude. "Thank your mother for me." He never told us his name. We saw him occasionally from afar, tending his sheep, but he did not speak to us again. He never returned the book, and we never asked him for it.

One day in late June Babcia went out to buy some food. She returned sooner than we expected, rushing into the shack, hugging and kissing us all.

"Mamusiu, have you gone crazy?" shouted Lala.

"We are free! We are free!" Babcia was shouting and jumping with joy. I had never seen an older person behave this way. "I heard in the store that Germany invaded Russia."

We all knew that Babcia's Russian was very poor, so nobody really believed her. Lila, who could speak Russian very well, ran to the store.

She came back, dancing one of her ballet steps. "It's true! It's true! Hitler is marching toward Moscow." I wasn't sure why everybody was so excited. How would this news make things better for us?

My mother explained, "Now that the Russians have to fight against Germany, they will have to free all their

Polish prisoners so we can help them fight."

Would we really be freed now? I was afraid to believe it. My mother had a small calendar, so I checked it to see what day it was: June 22, 1941.

Ivan knocked on the door and ordered us to the office. "An emergency meeting has been called."

This time I went with my mother and the other people from our shack. We went into a big room with white walls. This was the place where my mother had been interrogated so many times while I waited anxiously in the dark night, in our shack, fearing she would be arrested and I would never see her again. Natasha greeted us with a smile on her face. I had never seen her smile before.

"*Zdravstvuyte*, comrades, our friends. Our country is at war. We are all going to fight the same enemy. We have to work hard to provide food for the army."

What a change from her former speeches, I thought.

Unfortunately, she did not say that we were free to leave the kolkhoz, and we couldn't go anywhere without written permission. Everybody in Russia needed *udostovierenia* (documents) to travel from one place to another. And where would we go? We couldn't go home, because the Germans had already occupied Poland. Did the Russians expect us to stay here?

Even though we had been told we were "free," we continued to live in the same shack under the same conditions—with one big difference: there was no more banging on the door in the middle of the night. The NKVD no longer bothered us, and the officials now smiled and greeted us as equals. After work in the evenings, everybody would talk about leaving, but nobody could figure out how to do so or where to go. I thought often about how wonderful it would be to go back to Poland, but I knew this was impossible. As night fell we would pray together out loud: "Please, God, deliver us from this valley of sorrow, lead us to a free country where we will be able to live in peace." One voice, I think perhaps Babcia's, once added, "We need a miracle."

"Yes, yes," other voices joined in, "we do."

And then something that seemed miraculous did happen. Lila began talking with the manager of the store that usually had nothing to sell except toothpaste, perfume, and, occasionally, newspapers. Through him, she finally managed to obtain a newspaper that was more than a month old.

We gathered around her as she read out loud to us: "An Anglo-Soviet Treaty of Mutual Assistance was signed in Moscow on July 12, 1941. Stalin also signed an alliance with Britain's other ally, the Polish government in exile, in London on July 30, 1941. Under the latter agreement an amnesty was to be granted for the millions of innocent Polish deportees and prisoners in the USSR, and a new Polish army was to be formed in the depths of Russia. The command was to be given to General Anders, who was released from the Lyubianka prison."

We could hardly believe the words she read to us. Now we knew for sure that, after more than a year as political prisoners, we were free. My mother and I had just two things on our minds: finding Ciocia Stefa and my cousins Zosia and Nina, and finding a way to get out of Russia together.

PART IV

Flight to Freedom

12

Reunion and Departure

I heard loud knocking. As I ran to open the door of our shack I saw, in the shadows of the early evening, three silhouettes—thin, pale, and shabbily dressed.

"Who are you?" I gasped, jumping back.

Their sunken eyes stared back at me; their pallid lips tried to smile.

"Don't you recognize us?" One of the figures spoke. "It's Ciocia Stefa and your cousins Zosia and Nina."

"Mamusiu, come, come quickly!" I called.

My mother rushed to embrace them. They all began to cry.

"How did you get here?" my mother asked.

"We walked across the hills so the NKVD wouldn't see us. We didn't get permission to leave our kolkhoz.

We've been walking since the early morning, and we're very tired."

"Are you hungry?" Without waiting for a reply, my mother offered them some buckwheat soup and boiled potatoes. We watched them eat ravenously.

"This is a feast, a real feast," whispered Ciocia Stefa. "In our kolkhoz we could hardly get any food. We're happy to have survived this long."

We made room for them on our bunks. When they thought that Antek and I were asleep, they told terrible tales of their experiences. During the winter, 11 people had died of starvation in their hut, but the corpses couldn't be removed and buried, because of the snow, the frozen ground, and the wolves roaming outside. I listened in horror, careful not to make a sound so nobody would realize I could hear them.

Then Ciocia Stefa said, "We are free at last, but we must get out of the kolkhoz and move to a city where we can learn if Władzio is alive and out of prison."

My mother had a suggestion. "Tomorrow we will hire someone who has an ox-driven cart and go to Georgiewka. There is a government office that issues permits to move to another location. You know that in Russia nobody is allowed to travel freely."

I sat up in bed, no longer pretending to be asleep, and interrupted. "Mamusiu, will we also be able to look for Tatuś?"

My mother looked sad. "I'm sorry," she replied, "but we cannot. Remember that when we were taken out of

Lwów, he was hiding from the Russians. Now that the Germans are occupying Poland, we have no way of contacting any of our family for news of him. I'm afraid we'll have to wait until the end of the war to try to find him.

"All we can do," she continued, "is pray that we all survive and can be together again one day."

Early the next morning my mother, Ciocia Stefa, and Zosia left for Georgiewka. Nina stayed with Antek and me; she was only 17, but she knew how to take care of us. We loved Nina. She would tell us stories and sing to us. We didn't have any books, so her stories about Little Red Riding Hood and Sleeping Beauty were great entertainment. Antek, now six years old, especially adored her.

Three days later the travelers returned. Zosia told us, "We have all the papers in order, but we had to wait in line for hours to get them. The government is so slow." Ciocia Stefa announced, "Tomorrow we will go back to our kolkhoz, gather our belongings, and hire a cart to take us to a railway station. We'll head for the nearest city, Semipalatynsk, find accommodations, and wait for your arrival."

Once they left, we prepared for our departure. On a gray, overcast morning in late September, we packed our bundles and suitcases onto an oxcart. The Kazakh driver wore the customary round fur hat and gray coat, and the black hair of his beard was parted in the middle.

We traveled on the same bumpy, sandy road that had brought us here in May 1940, 16 months ago. Now we were no longer prisoners, but the road to complete freedom was not clear to us. Would we ever get out of Russia? I wondered.

We passed the hill and rocks where my baby sister was buried. I said a silent prayer: "We have to leave you here. We will never see you smile and grow up with us. May God and His angels look after you."

The slow movement of the cart put me to sleep. I awoke when I felt water on my face. It had stared to drizzle. I opened my little green umbrella, but my mother had only a woolen scarf to cover her head.

"Move closer to me, Antek," I instructed. I tried to cover both of us, but soon the drizzle developed into a steady rain that made our journey slower than anticipated. The visibility was poor. I knew that very soon the normally sun-scorched grasslands would turn into mud and we might get stuck on the road.

Darkness engulfed us, and we were still traveling. Near midnight we passed the dark shadows of some houses. No lights showed in any windows; the inhabitants were surely asleep. We heard the whistle of a train.

"Let's hope that's the Georgiewka railway station," my mother said.

Though it was still some distance away, voices were audible, and as we got nearer the noises grew louder. Soon a long building loomed before us. An oil lamp hung above the huge double door.

The cart stopped.

"*Vykhodite*," announced our driver, indicating that we should climb down. He helped us unload. I carried one suitcase, and my brother had a backpack. My mother had two suitcases.

"*Do svidania, spasibo*," she thanked the driver.

We walked into a big hall where very bright electric lights illuminated a crowd of people speaking a variety of languages: Russians, Kazakhs, Uzbeks, and Ukrainians. I even thought I heard some Polish. The hall was so full that we were crammed into one corner. We were wet, cold, tired, and hungry. The odor of sweaty, dirty bodies was overpowering, but we were glad to have a roof over our heads and no longer feel the rain falling on us.

I heard a voice calling, "Two rubles *kipiatok*, two rubles *kipiatok*." Many people rushed toward him.

"Stay here with Antek and don't move. Watch the suitcases," my mother said.

She took a big tin mug out of a bag and went to stand in line. I didn't know how much Antek understood of our situation, but he never complained. He cooperated and didn't stray from us.

When my mother came back she poured the hot water equally into smaller tin mugs and gave each of us a piece of dried bread that she had saved for our journey. The warm liquid helped take away the cold penetrating my body.

I fell asleep sitting on a suitcase, despite the glaring lights and the loud voices of Russian soldiers drinking vodka and singing a popular song: "*Vikhodila na biereg Katiusha, na vysokiy biereg nad rekoi*. Katiusha was waiting on a bank, on a high bank of a river."

The whistle of a train jerked me out of my sleep. But the train passed without stopping. My mother went to buy tickets and to ask about the schedule. She returned with bad news. "If a train is full, it doesn't stop. I don't know how long we will have to wait at this station."

The morning light penetrated the windows high above the hall. People started lining up on the platform. We moved outside, too, and tried to position ourselves so we would be able to get on a train if it stopped. After a couple of hours I heard a train approaching. "Please, God, let it stop," I prayed. It did stop, and the crowd pushed forward. At each door of the train stood a soldier holding a rifle and keeping anyone from boarding. The Russian soldiers waiting with us had priority; Hitler was marching toward Moscow, and the soldiers were going to the front to fight. No other passengers were allowed to board.

We sat on the platform all day. Three trains went by, one every two hours, and none of them stopped. From time to time we got up, stamped our feet, and waved our arms to keep warm.

"Children," my mother instructed, "the next time a train stops we have to push our way in. Krysiu, remember to hold Antek's hand tightly. Do not let go of him. I'll carry the luggage and I'll be right behind you as we move toward the door."

Finally, in the evening, one of the trains did stop. The doors opened, and a mass of bodies rushed forward. People shoved from all directions. Suddenly a tall, fat woman in a thick gray coat blocked my way. My face was pressed against her large bottom. In one hand I held Antek's hand and in the other my little umbrella. I thrust the umbrella into the woman's back. I doubted that she felt it through the thick fabric of her coat, but as she leaned toward the wagon's steps, I followed. At that moment a huge bundle of someone's belongings fell on our heads. My mother screamed, "*Dieti, dieti!* Children, children!" and pushed the bundle away with her hand. I was barely aware of what was going on behind me as I reached for the steps and pulled Antek. I managed to climb up into the train, pulling Antek with me, and we both fell into the dark passage, on top of the people already sitting there. "Watch out!" someone screamed. I stood up and then, squeezing between people, found a spot on the floor to sit down, hugging Antek closer to me.

The train started moving. I panicked. "Mamusiu, Mamusiu, where are you?"

I heard her voice. "I'm here. Don't worry."

I sighed in relief, even though I couldn't see her.

After many hours the morning light shone through the small window in the passage and I could see my mother, a few feet away, perched on our suitcases. Her dark-brown coat from Poland contrasted with the gray jackets worn by the two middle-aged women sitting next to her.

She smiled at me and Antek and said, "When we stop, listen carefully to the conductor's announcement. If he announces Semipalatynsk, then quickly get ready to leave and follow me."

I was exhausted. The rhythmic movement of the wheels put me to sleep. The conductor's voice woke me up: "Semipalatynsk, Semipalatynsk." I felt the train slowing down and stopping.

In an instant everyone around me moved and pressed toward the door. I didn't want to lose sight of my mother. I squeezed between two men, again pulling Antek with me. The pressure of the bodies practically threw us down the steps. My mother was standing on the platform, and we rushed to her.

People were leaving, and a new crowd was boarding the train. I looked around, hoping to see Zosia or Nina.

After a while I spotted someone waving and running toward us.

"Thank God you are here!" shouted Zosia. "We've been taking turns all week waiting for you at the station, watching every passing train. We found accommodations, and we gave our names to the Polish Committee, who will try to find our father."

Bending forward against the piercing gusts of cold wind, heads lowered, we walked out into the street. I felt so relieved that our journey was over—at least for now.

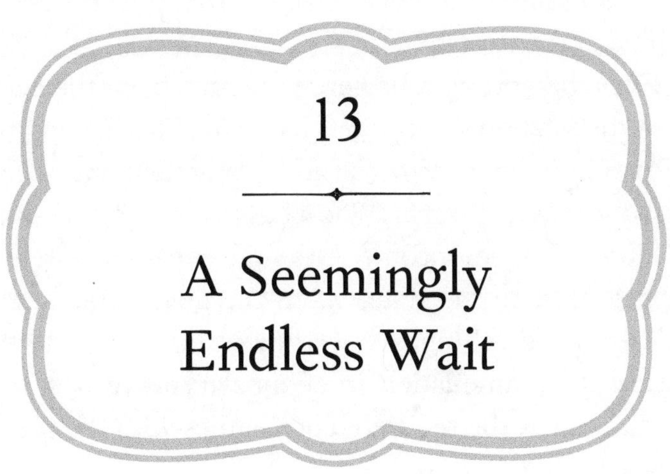

13

A Seemingly Endless Wait

My mother and Antek stretched their arms toward me, but I couldn't reach them. I felt glued to the platform, watching the train move farther and farther away from me. The crowd around me—Russian women in their colorful scarves tied under their chins, Kazakhs in their round fur hats, and Russian soldiers drinking vodka—were jeering and laughing.

"Stop the train!" I screamed. "Don't leave me. No! No!"

"Krysiu, Krysiu, wake up." My mother was shaking my arm. I opened my eyes. I was lying on a bed that faced a small window. She and Zosia, Nina, Ciocia Stefa, and Antek stood around the bed.

"I had a nightmare," I realized. "I thought you left me behind at the station."

Zosia had brought us here yesterday from the Semipalatynsk station. Ciocia Stefa had rented one room from a Russian woman who had four daughters and whose husband was in the army. She let us live with her in order to supplement her income. Although everything in Russia belonged to the state, when the government allotted her this dwelling, she was allowed to share it with others. Accommodation in Semipalatynsk was scarce, and as long as she registered our names with the police, nobody cared.

The room had beds made of wooden planks nailed into round legs that were stuck in the clay floor. The planks were long, so my mother, Antek, and I slept next to each other with our heads in the middle of the bed. Ciocia Stefa, Zosia, and Nina slept on the other end of the planks, in the opposite direction, our six heads meeting.

The Russian woman greeted us unsmilingly. "*Zdravstvuyte.*" Her graying hair was tied with a red scarf. Her large, stout figure and muscular arms showed that she was used to carrying heavy loads. She introduced her daughters in a deep, loud voice: "Svetlana, Katia, Nadia, and Natasha."

The daughters were all blonde with blue eyes. Svetlana was about 20 years old, tall and slim with a sulky expression. Katia, about 18, was short and plump. She nodded at us and walked away. Nadia was my age, about 10, and the only one who smiled at me. Natasha was 5, close to Antek's age. She jumped up and down as if ready to play and have some fun.

I didn't like to wake up in the mornings. I knew there was no food for breakfast. I would keep my eyes closed and imagine warm buns coming out of an oven. I would butter them and spread strawberry jam on them. This thought comforted me, but there was nothing to look forward to when, finally, I had to get out of bed.

My mother and either Zosia or Nina would go out and try to find food to buy. They waited in lines for hours but usually came back empty-handed. The war was on, and all the provisions were for the army and privileged officials. Another problem was that more and more refugees and evacuees were arriving from different parts of Russia. One day Ciocia Stefa and Zosia got temporary jobs packing potatoes and onions into bags and were able to bring home a few rations.

One evening we had only one slice of bread left, which we all shared. At night when we lay in bed head to head with the lights out, my mother suddenly cried out, "What are you doing, Stefa? Why are you poking my eye?"

"I'm sorry! I had a piece of bread that I wanted to give Any." That's what she always called my brother. Apparently she had hidden her share of the bread and was trying to stick it into my brother's mouth. But she missed it and stuck the bread into my mother's eye instead. We all laughed.

My brother was the only one who was ever invited to share a meal with the Russian family. Natasha liked

Antek, and her mother allowed her to share her portion of food with him. Antek told me that they both ate from one wooden bowl with wooden spoons. The soup consisted of hot water with a cabbage leaf, a small carrot, and sometimes potatoes. We were grateful that he could eat with them.

Before long we were in the middle of a very cold winter and still waiting for news about Wujcio Władzio. Every few days Zosia and Nina went to the Polish Committee to try to get some information, but they always returned with no news.

One day my mother took Antek and me with her to walk the streets of Semipalatynsk. On one corner, among the gray, drab-looking buildings, we saw a cart selling pickled green tomatoes packed into glass jars. My mother bought two. On another corner, an ice cream stand attracted our attention. Small rounds of ice cream were wrapped in gray paper. I was overjoyed when my mother bought me one, even though it tasted like cold water—it had no flavor and certainly no sugar. It was white, though, so I suppose it had some milk. It seemed strange to be selling ice cream when the temperatures were well below freezing, but any food was better than none.

By Christmas 1941 the streets of Semipalatynsk were frozen. Snow fell, and when the weather grew a little warmer, the snow melted, and then froze again when it got colder. As this process continued, eventually almost all the ground—the paths and the roads—hardened, turning the city into one large ice rink. People who had skates used them to get wherever they needed to go. Nadia was kind enough to let me borrow hers. We all wore *pimy* on our feet. The skates were fastened on tightly with strings. One day I was skating joyfully on the street in front of the gray brick house where we lived. Antek stood in the doorway, watching me jealously.

Suddenly someone grabbed my arms from behind my back. A young hooligan was cutting the strings while another held me firmly. I wanted to kick him but was afraid of the knife he was using. I felt powerless.

"Help! Help!" I screamed.

Antek ran for aid. In a minute the attackers were gone with the skates. Nadia and Katia rushed toward me. I was crying in despair and shaking with fear.

Katia was furious and started swearing. "*Svoloch, svoloch!* Animals, animals!"

Then she turned to Nadia, "Why did you lend your skates? How could you?"

Nadia's eyes filled with tears.

Then Katia looked at me. "I expect your mother to pay for the skates—do you hear me?"

"*Da, da,*" I sobbed.

I ran into the house, still crying, and told my mother the whole story. She tried to calm me. "It's all right, as long as they did not harm you. I'll find a way to pay Katia."

She gave her a sweater from Poland instead of money.

On Christmas Eve Ciocia Stefa covered the table with a white sheet, as we had no tablecloth. All we had for dinner was buckwheat soup and boiled potatoes. After we prayed and ate, we sang Christmas carols. Nina had a beautiful voice that carried across the room. She started with "Cicha noc," and we all joined in.

Suddenly four blonde heads popped into the doorway, watching us in astonishment. Religion was forbidden in Russia; the four girls had been brought up without knowing anything about God. I felt sorry for them, not knowing anything about Christmas, but I knew that I couldn't talk to them about Jesus being born on this day.

"*Pozhaluysta.* Come in." My mother invited them to sit with us and listen to our singing, without trying to explain anything.

They entered shyly and seemed to enjoy our company. When they left they thanked us, broad smiles on their faces.

At the end of February 1942 Zosia rushed in, shouting with excitement, "Good news! Our father is alive and well! He is in the Polish army in Yangi Yul, Uzbekistan, under the command of General Anders. I asked the Polish Committee to send him a letter to let him know where we are."

We started kissing each other and crying. Our joy that day could not be described in words.

Two weeks later a short letter arrived.

My dearest. I was so happy to hear from you. As soon as possible I will send somebody to Semipalatynsk with papers allowing you to join me here in Yangi Yul, Uzbekistan. Love to you all,
Władzio

The next few weeks dragged by as we waited impatiently for more news. My mother and Ciocia Stefa dried slices of dark bread for the journey.

One day toward the end of March, there was a knock on the door. Nina opened it to reveal a short middle-aged man in a green military uniform that hung loosely on his thin body.

He took off his hat and said, "I am looking for the Balicki family. I am Sergeant Borowski. I come with papers from Captain Doctor Balicki. We must leave as soon as possible or we may miss the transport to Persia that is departing shortly." (As my uncle's official title was doctor of law, the polite way to address him was Doctor.)

"What about us?" cried my mother. "I am her sister, and I have two children."

"I know about you," Sergeant Borowski replied. "The problem is that I was only able to obtain papers for the immediate family, who will be recruited into the army. You may also join, but your children are underage. I have no permission to take them with me. I'll come back tomorrow, and we will talk about it."

After he left, my mother and cousins debated late into the night. I listened until I fell asleep, so I didn't hear the end of the discussion. The next morning my mother announced, "We have to leave without permits."

"It's too risky. The police will arrest you," argued Ciocia Stefa.

When Sergeant Borowski returned later that day, my mother told him her decision. He scratched his head and grew silent. Finally, he spoke. "I have an idea. I will add you and your children to the list. We will write down that your daughter is 25 years old and your son 20. They will have to hide when the police come to check people on the train. God help us if they discover our fraud!"

The next day my mother woke up and reported one of her prophetic dreams. "I had a strange dream," she said. "Nina, wearing a black dress, walked onto a stage with a black background. She was going to sing. A huge white hand appeared behind her, and a voice whispered, "*Zaczekać, zaczekać*. Wait, wait."

"You and your dreams," laughed Zosia. "Let's go."

We gathered our belongings and walked to the station. The pavements were muddy from the thawing snow, and the early spring air was cold and crisp.

All we could do now was pray, and hope for the best.

14

The Trans-Siberian Train Journey

The seven of us—my mother, Antek, Ciocia Stefa, Zosia, Nina, and me, plus Sergeant Borowski, who would inquire about the train schedule and buy our tickets—arrived at the train station in Semipalatynsk to find it crowded with Russians, Kazakhs, and Poles going south. The German army was advancing toward Moscow, so the trains that passed by the station without stopping were full to capacity with refugees and evacuees from other parts of Russia. The possibility of boarding any of them seemed grim.

We were careful not to be seen with Sergeant Borowski at the ticket booth when he presented the papers allowing us to travel. As planned, he had forged our ages, declaring on our permits that my brother was 20 and I was 25, instead of our true ages of 7 and 11.

Pushing our way to the platform, we tried to get as close as possible to the rails so we would be in a good position to board the train when it pulled into the station. We didn't dare lose our place, for fear of being left behind in the rush of hopeful passengers. The icy-cold weather penetrated our thin clothing, but all we could do to keep warm was stamp our feet and move our arms. Around us people were huddled together in clusters, surrounded by cardboard boxes and bundles wrapped in blankets and sheets. We all waited, staring down the empty tracks as hour after hour passed. Darkness was starting to fall when we finally heard the whistle of an engine.

The sight of the approaching train sparked the listless mass into a raging mob. The station turned into a surge of people shoving and clawing their way toward the opening train doors.

I saw Nina climbing into a window. My mother handed Antek to her. Ciocia Stefa and Zosia pushed me from behind at Sergeant Borowski, who was already on the steps. He stretched out his arms and pulled me onto the train. We forced our way into an overcrowded passage as people swore at us. Finally, I curled up into a corner on the floor and held tightly to my suitcase, fearing that if I let go, it would be stolen.

The wagon shook and started rolling with a squeak. At last we were on our way. I let out a sigh of relief as I listened to the rhythmic turning of the wheels and tried hard not to fall asleep, but failed.

Morning came. The first sight that met my eyes was two middle-aged Russian women wearing the traditional short gray quilted coats and flowery scarves tied under their chins. They were sitting opposite me, and, to my horror, I saw tiny, short white threads moving up and down their clothing: lice were crawling all over them. My mother saw this, too, and took a small bag from her purse. She started sprinkling a white powder over us, which also spread over the floor.

The door from the adjoining railway car opened and a conductress appeared, yelling at the top of her voice: "Tickets! Tickets!" She wore a navy uniform over her stout figure and carried a leather bag over her shoulder. Her graying hair was tied at the back of her head; her tired-looking blue eyes scrutinized every passenger. Sergeant Borowski handed her our tickets, which she clipped without comment. She didn't seem to care how the tickets had been obtained, as long as everybody was accounted for.

As she passed by us, however, she noticed the white powder. "What's this?" she demanded.

My mother replied: "This is to prevent getting lice."

The conductress shook her head and pointed to her forehead. *"Polaki, duraki,"* she said, indicating she thought Poles were idiots.

My mother followed her and whispered something. I saw the conductress nodding her head. I also noticed

This photo of my mother was taken in 1942. I think it shows both her determination and her sense of humor.

her slipping something into her leather bag. Later I realized that my mother's gold watch was gone. Why was my mother bribing this woman? I wondered.

When we came to the next big station and people started leaving the train, I understood. The conductress motioned us toward a vacated compartment before anybody else could occupy it. The compartment consisted of two wooden benches facing each other, with wide shelves for storing luggage above them.

The train started moving, slowly at first, and then soaring down the metal-and-wood-ribbed rails, across the barren countryside of Kazakhstan. We passed some small railway stations where crowds were waiting, but the train made only brief stops at them, taking off without any signal or warning. Eventually I dozed off to the sound of the wagon spinning and clicking.

On the morning of our third day of traveling, the cessation of movement interrupted my sleep. The train had come to a stop. A voice outside announced loudly, "Alma Ata, Alma Ata."

Everybody was curious to see the view outside. An awe-inspiring sight met our eyes. The rays of the rising sun, which was still hidden from us in the valley, lit the snowy peaks of high mountains. The belt of light widened to the lower regions, but the city itself was still filled with darkness. Only the station had lamps, illuminating the waiting crowds.

Then Zosia shouted, "Look out! The NKVD is getting on the train."

"Calm down, calm down," said Sergeant Borowski. "Hide the children. I'll deal with the police."

Zosia grabbed Antek and lifted him onto the luggage rack above our seats. She covered him with a blanket and threw some bags on top of him. My mother pushed me under one of the wooden benches and blocked the opening with a small suitcase. The space had probably never been cleaned; the dirt and dust were choking me, but I didn't dare utter a sound. It seemed like an eternal wait until I heard a deep, loud voice in the corridor: "Papers, identification, permits." I heard the door open and could only guess that Sergeant Borowski was handing over the forms as he explained, "We are all going to join the Polish army in Yangi Yul."

The voice said, "Where are the two other people listed here on the papers?" My heart stood still, and my body tensed.

"Please help us, God," I prayed silently.

"They stepped out to buy some food and water at the station," Sergeant Borowski lied. "They will be back shortly."

What is going to happen now? I thought.

"*Khorosho.* Fine," the voice answered.

The door closed. I sighed with relief. Was it over?

"The children must stay hidden until the police leave the train," Sergeant Borowski said harshly.

But the NKVD didn't leave. The train started up again and gained speed while I lay on the cold steel floor. I felt every movement of the squeaking and shaking wheels. I didn't dare to come out. After about an hour the train slowed down and came to a stop.

"Frunze, Frunze," the name of the station was announced.

When the train stopped in Alma Ata, the capital city of Kazakhstan, my brother and I had to hide from the NKVD police. © *Ilya Postnikov/Dreamstime.com*

"The NKVD is getting off the train!" my mother cried.

I climbed out from under the bench. Antek was already sitting on it, and my mother was passing out the small pieces of dry dark bread that she had prepared for the journey. The air was stuffy because the windows were jammed shut. The wagons were very old and badly maintained.

Toward evening we saw the flickering lights of a city. As the train stopped, the announcement came from the platform: "Tashkent, Tashkent."

"This is the capital of Uzbekistan," explained Sergeant Borowski. "Very soon we'll reach Yangi Yul. It's a small station, and the train may not stop there long. We will have to move quickly."

About an hour later we reached Yangi Yul. As we disembarked from the train, the first thing we saw was a Polish soldier wearing a green beret emblazoned with an eagle. He was marching up and down the platform, carrying a rifle. Ciocia Stefa ran to him. "Do you know of Doctor Balicki, my husband, attached to General Anders's military court?"

"Yes, I met him. He left three days ago for Persia with a transport of soldiers."

When we heard these words, we were in shock, not believing our ears. Completely crestfallen, we sat down on our suitcases. What would our fate be now?

Sergeant Borowski shook his head and said, "I'm so sorry. I cannot do anything more for you."

Suddenly a jeep stopped near us. A young blonde woman in a short green skirt and military jacket jumped out. She looked at us, and then Zosia called out, "Do you remember me? We went to high school together!"

They embraced warmly, and Zosia asked, "Have you seen our father? The soldier told us that he left for Persia."

"That's not true! I saw him this morning," the blonde woman answered. "I don't have permission to take passengers in a military vehicle, so I can't take you to him in this car. But I'll let him know you are here. I am part of the PAWC—the Polish Auxiliary Women's Corps—and I hope that you'll be joining us."

Soon after she left we saw a man of medium height, wearing a military uniform, approaching us. It was my uncle! I recognized his walk, but he was much thinner than I remembered. Two years of prison life had taken their toll on him. Ciocia Stefa started walking toward him. We all stood still, watching silently along with the other people around us. My aunt and uncle fell into each other's arms, crying.

Then Wujcio Władzio embraced everybody else, except for me. "Where is Krysia?" he asked.

"I'm right here, Wujcio."

"I didn't recognize you! You've grown so much!" Before him stood a thin girl wearing brown mismatched boots that my mother had managed to get for me. Antek stood beside me in green-laced shoes. The sleeves of my shabby coat were too short, and Antek's jacket barely fit him, either. We must have looked very different from the well-fed, well-dressed children he remembered.

"I've rented two rooms with a Russian family, and I have a car waiting that General Anders kindly let me use tonight. My orders were to leave for Persia, but I knew you were coming and managed to get off the list."

We packed into the jeep, and the military driver took us through the dark streets. Though we were still on Soviet soil, I felt indescribably relieved to know the Polish army was so near.

15

Tragedy Strikes Home

"We're joining the Polish army," announced Zosia. She, Nina, and Ciocia Stefa left for work at the army headquarters. My mother, Antek, and I remained in the Russian family's house where Wujcio Władzio had rented rooms for us.

The house was on a narrow street with high mud walls marked only by wooden doors that led to houses with interior courtyards. Built from sand-colored clay, it was U-shaped, so all the doors and windows overlooked the courtyard. We lived in two adjoining rooms with a small entrance hall in which a stove for burning wood or coal to heat the area stood against one wall. There were two beds in the smaller room and three in the larger, which also held two benches and a small table.

All of the furnishings were made from wooden planks with a rough finish. By now we were quite accustomed to primitive life and happy to have a roof over our heads.

One day the Russian family from whom we rented the rooms must have been at work, because only an old woman and a small boy about Antek's age were in the courtyard. The woman was washing clothing in a tin bucket, and the boy was jumping around.

Antek could speak Russian very well by now; he had learned the language quickly from the Russian children in Kazakhstan. He went to the boy and asked him his name. "Yuri," the boy replied, with a smile. They started chasing each other around the courtyard. I was glad Antek had company.

In the evening Ciocia Stefa, Wujcio Władzio, Zosia, and Nina came home, all wearing dark-green military uniforms. They brought rations given to them—dried meat and some bread—which they were going to share with us.

"When do you think we will be able to get out of Russia?" my mother asked.

"I don't know," replied Wujcio Władzio. "Nobody knows anything, not even General Anders. The Russians are very slow in issuing permits and organizing transportation. I heard a rumor that we might go to China instead of Persia. All we can do is wait. A Polish school was started not far from here, and Krysia should attend."

The next day my mother, Antek, and I walked across the vineyards toward a small, rectangular red-brick building with a veranda in front, nestled under a cluster of trees. A young, slender woman was sitting on a chair, reading a story in Polish to a crowd of children resting on the grass in front of her. She got up and greeted us.

"*Dzień dobry.* Good morning. I am Maria Dombrowska. I was a teacher in Poland, and now I am the only one teaching the Polish children here. We don't have books, paper, or pencils for every child, but I teach from the few books that I was able to obtain. We play games and sing. Sister Teresa teaches religion three times a week."

"This is my daughter, Krystyna," my mother said. "May I please leave her with you?"

"Yes, of course."

My mother left, and I found a space to sit on the grass. It turned out that the building was reserved for the military administration, and, as far as I could understand, we weren't allowed to go inside. I looked around. Most of the children were younger than me, except for two older girls whom the teacher called Alina and Ewa.

I found the class boring. All the stories and songs were aimed at the younger children. After a very simple lesson Pani Maria announced, "Class dismissed."

I walked home across fields full of early spring flowers blooming purple and yellow. I longed for the day when I would be able to go to a regular school and resume my studies. A few Uzbek women in their native garb of pantaloons and multicolored blouses passed me without greetings or smiles. I was used to seeing them every day, carrying babies on their backs or, on their heads, piles of branches neatly tied together with string. Under the shade of a tree, the Uzbek men sat talking and laughing. Some looked old, but most of them were young. I guessed that they were laborers working in the vineyards, resting after picking grapes all day.

My uncle was a judge attached to the military court, and one day he had to travel to Samarkand, a large city in Uzbekistan. He came back with a strange tale.

"Now I understand why the Uzbeks are so well disposed toward Poles," he related. "In the 12th century, in the southern city of Kraków, a trumpet fanfare was played every hour from the top of the spire of Saint Mary's church. When the city was invaded by the Tatars of the Golden Horde, the sentry trumpeted the warning—'Hejnal'—but was abruptly interrupted by an arrow shot through his throat by one of Genghis Khan's cavalrymen. Over the centuries the story has been told here in the steppes, along with a prophecy that until a Polish trumpeter plays 'Hejnal' on Uzbek soil, Uzbekistan will not be free of Russian domination. The Uzbeks are very superstitious, so they asked the Polish authorities to have somebody play it from the top of one of the mosques—against protests from the Russian authorities, of course. One day," he concluded, "when we go back to Poland, we will tell everybody about this."

One of the most important holidays in Poland is May 3, Dzień Konstytucji, which commemorates the day the Polish Constitution was written in 1791. The Polish army decided to celebrate this holiday with a show, and Nina was one of the singers. The stage was set outside on a raised wooden platform. First Nina and two other girls in uniform performed a chorus. They were followed by two men who told jokes that everybody laughed at, except me, since I didn't understand the adult humor. Then Nina took the stage alone. She sang "Ostatni mazur" ("The Last Mazur")—the song about a young man asking his girlfriend for one last mazurka dance before he goes off to war, the same song my parents danced to the night they met. She sang like a lark. The sun shone brightly on her light-brown hair, and her voice rang out across the audience. Everyone clapped their hands in delight.

In this photo taken in 1940, just before we were deported from Poland, my then 15-year-old cousin Nina has a sad look in her eyes, as though she knows what the future holds.

Three months passed, and we were still waiting for a transport to take us out of Russia. One day in late May 1942 my mother and I were trying to walk the streets of Yangi Yul toward a market that had little to sell but where we could sometimes barter for bread or grapes. This time we could not get through to the market. Evacuees and refugees from other parts of Russia crowded the city, escaping the German army that was advancing toward Moscow. There weren't enough accommodations for all of them, so many were living on the streets. The heat was so intense and the sun so scorching that most people tied sheets or blankets from one side of a building to another to try to create a little shade. The stench of human waste was sickening. Piles of garbage were everywhere, covered by swarms of buzzing flies.

June also went by without a word from the authorities about our leaving Russia. Meanwhile, the lack of adequate sanitation contaminated the water supplies, causing an epidemic of dysentery, typhoid, and typhus to break out. It was only a matter of time before one of these diseases reached our family: Ciocia Stefa and Nina both came down with typhus. For two long weeks they lay ill at home while my mother did her best to nurse them. I helped by keeping the flies away from Nina's face. She was so sick that most of the time she didn't even recognize me. Ciocia Stefa was just as sick, but she was more coherent.

My mother wanted me to go to school every day so that I wouldn't be exposed to the disease any more than necessary. One day I came home from school to find both Ciocia Stefa and Nina gone.

"Where are they?" I asked.

"They were taken to the hospital," my mother sadly replied.

For the next two weeks I continued going to school every day. Sister Teresa was preparing us to receive the sacrament of confirmation. She had been a nun in Poland, but one day she had been arrested on the street and deported to Russia. Two years of prison had left a mark on her. She was short, with a sallow complexion and dark-brown eyes. Nobody could guess her age. She could have been in her early forties or much younger. She couldn't get a veil to cover her head in Russia, so she hid her hair under a short blue scarf tied at the back of her head, with one end hanging out.

At home we did nothing but worry about Ciocia Stefa and Nina. We weren't allowed to visit, because they were in isolation, but every day my mother or Zosia would go to the hospital to get an update on their medical conditions. Every effort was being made to save Nina because she was young, but Ciocia Stefa did not get much treatment, because the nurses said she was "*starukha*, an old woman." She was 44 years old.

The confirmation date was set for July 14. That morning Wujcio Władzio went to the hospital and then quickly returned, crying. "Nina's condition is critical. I am going back to the hospital. Zosia is already waiting there."

"I'm coming with you!" my mother sobbed.

"Mama, what about me! I have to go for confirmation."

"You go alone, and Antek will stay here with the Russian family. Children aren't allowed in the hospital."

So I walked sadly across the fields, in the blistering July heat, toward the Polish army barracks. A crowd of soldiers and civilians gathered for the ceremony on a grass-covered area used for military training. I found my group with Sister Teresa.

"Do you have a sponsor?" she asked me.

"No, I'm alone." I didn't give her any explanation.

"I will be your sponsor. What name are you going to take?"

I thought for a moment. "I will be Teresa."

Sister Teresa smiled and nodded in agreement. Little did she know that I didn't care about my confirmation name, or anything else. I could only think about my family waiting in anguish at the hospital.

Everyone who was going to be confirmed stood in a row. General Anders marched in and positioned himself in the line with us. I wondered why he was here. Then I heard somebody behind me whisper, "He is also going to be confirmed because he converted to Catholicism." Then I remembered Wujcio Władzio mentioning that the general had recently been baptized.

A bishop I had never seen before appeared. He wore military attire because church attire was not available in Russia. He was tall and thin, with graying hair. He looked just like everybody else who had suffered two years of malnutrition in prison. The only reason I even knew he was a bishop was that I knew priests could not perform confirmation. A priest carrying a tin bowl filled with oil accompanied him.

The ceremony began.

The bishop intoned, "Do you believe in the Father, God Almighty?"

"I do," the crowd answered.

"Do you renounce Satan and all his evil works?"

"I do."

"Do you, do you, do you?"

"I do, I do, I do," I answered automatically, without comprehending anything being said. All I wanted was for the ceremony to be over so I could go home to find out about Nina.

The bishop walked to each person in turn. When he came to me, Sister Teresa put her hand on my right shoulder.

"Who is sponsoring you, my child?"

"I am," answered Sister Teresa.

"And what name are you taking?"

"Teresa," I replied.

The bishop dipped his two fingers into the bowl of oil and made the sign of the cross on my forehead. "I confirm you in your faith *in Nomine Patris et Filii, et Spiritus Sancti*, in the name of the Father, and of the Son, and of the Holy Spirit. Amen." He extended his hand toward me. I knew I was supposed to kiss the holy relics embedded in the stone on his ring.

The ceremony ended, and the crowd dispersed. I walked home as fast as I could. When I came through the door I was met by a deadly silence. Where was everybody?

"Is anybody home?" I cried out.

My mother came out of the other room, very pale, and embraced me tightly. I knew without her telling me what had happened. Nina was gone. I would never see her again. A terrible feeling of loss shook my entire body. I began screaming. My mother held me until I calmed down, and then I sobbed quietly on her shoulder.

The next day I overheard Wujcio Władzio tell my mother, "The funeral is tomorrow morning. I think Krysia should not attend. It's going to be too hard on the child. Let her go to school." I was very upset, but I knew I couldn't go against my uncle's wishes.

The next day, during the short school break, sitting on the grass I heard Alina say to Ewa, "Today is the funeral of one of the PAWC."

I started crying. "It's my cousin. She died."

"My sister also died," said Alina sadly.

"My aunt, too," whispered Ewa.

Pani Maria overheard us and said, "Every day somebody dies. Let's resume class."

Was her remark supposed to make me feel better? I thought bitterly. Was that all the sympathy I was going to get? Nina was not just anybody. She was young, kind, and beautiful. She wasn't even 18 years old. I couldn't believe I would never hear her sing again. I already missed her terribly.

After class I headed home with a heavy heart. I found the house full of gloom. Everybody was back from the funeral. Wujcio Władzio had locked himself in one of the bedrooms. Zosia was somewhere in the garden, alone. My mother was sitting on the bed with Antek, who looked terribly sad. I knew that he understood far more than we realized, but he never expressed his feelings. He had been Nina's favorite; she had loved him so much. I knew he was missing her, too.

Nina was buried in this grave in Yangi Yul, Uzbekistan, in July 1942.

"Why didn't you take me to the funeral?" I demanded.

"It was too painful," said my mother. "I didn't want you to go through that pain. I want you to remember Nina the way she was before she became ill. She had a military funeral; taps were played, and shots were fired."

"Mamusiu, do you remember the dream you had before we left Semipalatynsk?" I asked her. "The one where Nina walked onto a black stage dressed in a dark dress and a large white hand behind her waved while a voice said, '*Zaczekać, zaczekać*'?"

"Unfortunately, my dreams always come true," my mother answered. "But it was God's will. Now Nina is singing with the angels. Let's hope now that Ciocia Stefa gets better."

The three of us embraced and sat crying quietly together.

Two more weeks passed, and we were still in Uzbekistan, still waiting to get out.

16

Setting Sail for Freedom at Last

The tragedy of Nina's death and the threat of not getting out of Russia made life at home unbearable. We barely spoke to one another. Wujcio Władzio and Zosia left the house every morning for work at the army headquarters, and I went to school. Sometimes I didn't go, and my mother didn't force me. I couldn't stop thinking about Nina and how much I missed her. When Zosia returned in the evenings, she would kneel down and pray. Her hazel eyes had lost their laughing sparkle. She no longer smiled, and she stopped telling us stories from her childhood in Poland. She had been just one and a half years older than Nina; the two of them had been like twins. They understood each other, they enjoyed doing things together, and I had never heard them quarrel.

The day finally came when Wujcio Władzio came home and announced, "The first transport will be leaving soon for Krasnovodsk on the way to Persia, across the Caspian Sea. The Russian authorities are allowing only three departures from Yangi Yul." Ciocia Stefa was still in the hospital and too weak to travel, so we would be the last to leave, he explained.

"No, no," my mother cried. "Please, Władzio, use your influence to get permission for me and the children to go first. You, Stefa, and Zosia are in the army and you will be allowed to leave, but the children and I might not be so lucky. If one of us gets ill with one of the diseases going around, we might miss the date of departure and we'll have to stay in Russia forever."

"You're right," Wujcio Władzio agreed. "I'll do my best to get you on that first list."

A week later he came home with good news. "Get ready. You and the children can leave in three days. The only problem is that the Russians cannot provide passenger coaches, so you will have to travel in cattle wagons."

"We arrived in Russia in cattle wagons, and we'll leave the same way!" my mother shouted with joy. "As long as we get out of this God-forsaken country!"

We didn't have much to pack. Everything fit into our two suitcases, plus each of the three of us wore a backpack. My mother dried some dark bread for the journey, knowing that we would not be able to obtain any other food on the trip.

Wujcio Władzio got permission to transport us to the station in a military jeep. When we got there, a long chain of cattle wagons was waiting. Russian and Polish military personnel stood by, holding the lists of people who were allowed to leave. We went over to one of the Polish soldiers, who directed us to a wagon. Another soldier helped each of us climb up into the wide opening.

Wujcio Władzio and Zosia, who had also accompanied us to the station, looked at us with concern.

"Don't worry!" my mother called to them. "We'll see you soon in Persia." I couldn't believe that soon we would no longer be under the control of the Russians.

More and more people kept arriving. After almost an hour the whistle blew and the train started moving slowly. Before a soldier shut the big door of our wagon, we waved good-bye to Wujcio Władzio and Zosia. The shaking and rattling grew steadily stronger as the train picked up speed, heading in the direction of freedom.

There were no benches inside the wagon; we sat on our suitcases. There was a wooden bunk along one wall, and some people were already climbing onto it to get a view through the two small, high windows. The stench of cow manure filled the air. The people inside were mostly women and children of various ages, plus two old men who were so weak they couldn't stand up without help.

I spotted a brown-haired girl in one corner. She looked at me with dark-blue eyes framed by long black lashes, and we recognized each other: it was Ewa from my

Polish school in Yangi Yul. We had never become friends, because she was two years older than me—almost 14—but now I was glad to have her company. We smiled at each other, and after a while she made her way toward me, pushing through people and bundles of luggage.

"I didn't know that you would be traveling today," she said. "Mamusia said that it would take us about two days to reach Krasnovodsk. There are no toilet facilities, so I hope we'll be allowed to stop at some stations."

After a few hours the train did stop, and a Polish soldier opened the door. "*Proszę wychodzić.* Please come out."

I looked out. The evening was very dark, and there was no sign of any station. I jumped down, and then I realized that people were relieving themselves next to their wagons. So that was the reason the train had stopped in the middle of nowhere.

That first night we slept on our suitcases. I awoke to the morning light drifting through the small windows and looked up at the people sitting high on the bunk. A young woman with short blonde hair and smiling eyes must have guessed from my expression that I wanted to see the countryside.

"Would you like to see where we are now?" she asked me.

"Yes, please."

Stretching out her hand, she pulled me up onto the wooden bunk. I looked out at an immense desert of pale-yellow waves. The sands rolled toward the horizon, melting into the grayish-blue skyline. The rays of the rising sun shone brightly over the vast wilderness. A caravan of camels in the far distance was the only sign of life.

"We crossed into Turkmenistan and are now traveling across the Kyzylkum Desert, north of Persia and west of Afghanistan," explained the young woman. "I'm so glad that I still remember my geography lessons from Poland," she laughed.

I thanked her for letting me see the view, and slid down the bunk so that others could climb up and have their turns at the window.

Around noon we stopped again. The door opened, and two Polish soldiers and one Russian soldier entered with buckets of water. We had long ago learned to travel with tin mugs, and now we filled them with the water. My mother gave Antek and me pieces of the dried bread she had packed, and we dipped them into the water to soften them. We were allowed to leave the wagon to stretch our legs. Again we had to use the railway lines as toilets, which was very embarrassing, especially in daylight, but once again we had stopped in the middle of nowhere. I remembered that the bathrooms in Russian railway stations were filthy and overcrowded, so I understood why our train wasn't stopping at any of them.

On the third day, late in the evening, we arrived at our destination. I heard the doors opening and voices outside shouting, "Krasnovodsk, Krasnovodsk!"

Grabbing our luggage, we jumped down onto sandy soil. I didn't see any station. Where are we? I wondered.

I felt a slight breeze on my face and heard the sound of splashing water. I guessed we must be near the Caspian Sea. Polish and Russian soldiers were carrying oil lamps that provided a dim light. They motioned the crowd of waiting people to move forward. We followed them and then were stopped.

"Wait here. All papers have to be checked," one of the soldiers ordered.

I sank onto the sand and fell asleep with my head on my backpack. Soon I felt my mother shaking my arm. "Get up. We have to go."

I roused myself and, taking Antek's hand, followed her. Walking in the sand was so tiring that I took off my brown sandals. Why couldn't this wait until morning? It seemed like everything in Russia had to be done at night. Then I remembered that every step brought us closer to freedom.

Finally, we reached a small hut of corrugated iron, with a passage in the middle where the NKVD and Polish soldiers were waiting. Every permit was thoroughly scrutinized by both parties. After we passed through the opening to the other side, we walked for some distance in total darkness until the Polish soldier leading us shouted, *"Stanąć!"* We obeyed, stopping, and waited there for the rest of the night.

With the first rays of daylight, rusty gray buildings became visible in the near distance. We were at the port of Krasnovodsk. The green waves of the Caspian Sea stretched to the blue horizon. I knew that it was really a huge lake, but because of its size, it was called a sea. Two ships were in the harbor, and maintenance crews dressed in gray overalls worked on the ship decks.

I heard somebody say that one of the ships was an oil tanker. Which one was our ticket to freedom? I wondered.

"Kontrola, kontrola," came a voice from the crowd. The NKVD in their dark-blue uniforms were ordering people to open their bags and suitcases for inspection. I didn't know what they were looking for.

My mother grabbed her little leather bag that held some jewelry and photos of my father and handed it to me without a word. I understood. I pressed the bag against my chest and grabbed my brother's hand, and we both walked a little distance away from all the people, pretending to play in the sand with our feet. We stayed away until the NKVD passed my mother, and then we returned to her. We had no idea what they had been looking for or why.

The day dragged on, the merciless sun burning our backs. The air was humid, with very little breeze from the sea.

An old woman wearing a faded brown dress was sitting on the ground with her back against her suitcase. Her gray hair was tied at the back with a piece of black ribbon, and her thin hands were clasped in front of her. Her eyes were closed, and I assumed she was sleeping. A Polish soldier was walking about, checking on people. He noticed the woman and touched her arm. She didn't move. He called, *"Szybko, szybko, pomoc!* Quick, quick, help!" Another soldier came running.

The two of them carried her away as the people standing around shook their heads sadly. I realized that she had died on the threshold of freedom. At that moment I also knew that I would never forget her.

At sunset I noticed some activity. Russian soldiers on horses were approaching the harbor, riding toward the oil tanker. As they passed by us, a Polish soldier announced, "The soldiers are going to the other side of the Caspian Sea to Baku, where large supplies of oil are concentrated. The Germans need the oil, so it has to be well guarded. After they finish boarding it will be our turn. We will start loading the other Soviet freighter."

Another hour passed before we began moving forward. The NKVD and Polish representatives stood by the gangplanks, checking lists of names. Every once in a while a Russian official would ask somebody to step aside and a Polish soldier would try to explain the problem to the prospective passenger.

Fear contracted the muscles in my arms and legs. I recognized the feeling; it was the same fear that I had felt when the NKVD came to arrest us in our home in Poland, and the same emotion that had overwhelmed me in Kazakhstan when they wanted to take Antek and me away from our mother and put us in an orphanage. Would we be able to pass onto the ship? What if we were not allowed to leave? The next few steps toward freedom felt like the longest walk of my life.

When our turn came, my mother said, "*Familia* Mihulka."

The NKVD soldier scanned the list, nodded, and motioned us forward. "*Davai*. Go."

My grip on my mother's hand relaxed as we continued walking up the wooden plank until we reached the deck. We found a spot in the middle of the boat, next to a wooden pole, and watched as more and more people

This Soviet freighter groaned under the weight of the refugees ready to sail across the Caspian Sea to freedom. For all I know, I might have been among those on this very ship. *Photo courtesy of Franek Rymaszewski*

came on board, filling up all the space until there was hardly any room to spare.

At last the plank was lifted in preparation for departure. It was a moonless night; the only lights were some dim oil lamps at the front and back of the ship. I looked at the pale faces surrounding me, the poorly clad, half-starved bodies. Some people were praying; some were crying. I wondered if they were tears of hope and joy, or tears of sorrow at the graves they had left behind. I thought about my baby sister's grave on the steppes of Kazakhstan and my cousin Nina, buried in a military cemetery in Yangi Yul.

The boat moved. Complete silence fell over the crowd. The only sound was the splash of waves hitting against the sides of the ship. The flicker of lights in the Krasnovodsk port was our last sight of the land where we had suffered so deeply. Soon they faded into the distance.

In the stillness of the night a song spontaneously arose from the crowd—the Polish national anthem: "*Jeszcze Polska nie zginęła pòki my żyjemy!* Poland is not lost so long as we still live!"

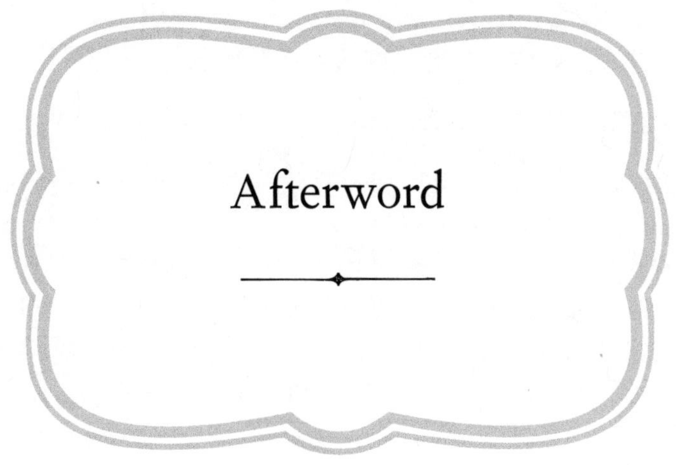

Afterword

In spite of all the amnesties and agreements, Stalin did not keep his word. Not long after we left the USSR, all permits and transports were stopped. More than 1.5 million people had been deported from their homes in eastern Poland; only about 130,000 of these deportees made it out of Russia. What happened to the others? Half of them died in labor camps and prisons or simply vanished, some were drafted into the Russian army, and a small number returned to Poland after the war. Those of us who made it out of Russia were the lucky ones.

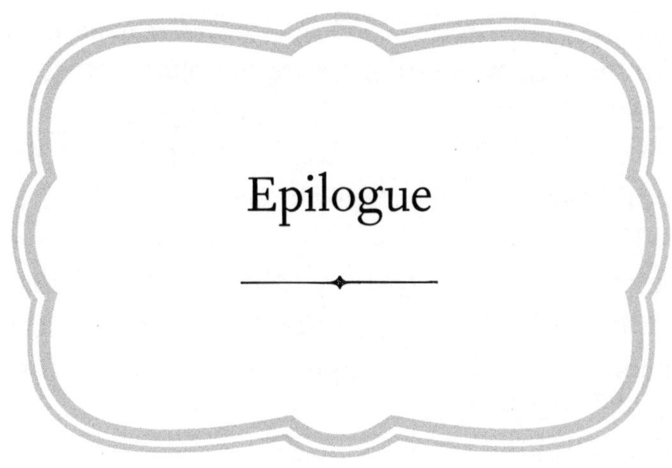

Epilogue

After our boat left Krasnovodsk, we sailed all night and day until we reached Pahlavi, Persia. For a month we lived on the beach. Our next home was a refugee camp in a park that had been a residence of one of the shah's wives, in Persia's capital, Tehran. Now it was filled with tents, and we settled into one of them.

Not long after, Ciocia Stefa, Wujcio Władzio, and Zosia arrived. Zosia soon left to travel with the army to Lebanon and Italy, while Ciocia Stefa and Wujcio Władzio remained until 1943, when they followed Zosia. In May 1944 my mother, Antek, and I were sent to Africa to await the end of the war. My mother was assigned to a medical team in Northern Rhodesia, and so we joined the 1,000 people at Bwana M'Kubwa, the

Polish refugee camp there. My mother worked in the pharmacy, my brother went to the camp school, and I was sent to Dominican Convent High School, a boarding school in Ndola where I learned English.

The war finally ended in May 1945. To our dismay, we learned about a secret meeting in December 1943 between the United States, England, and Russia. The three countries had agreed to keep Poland under Soviet control in exchange for Soviet participation in the war against Japan. The Polish Communist government announced that anyone who did not return to Poland by a certain date would be deprived of citizenship. We were not willing to live under Communism, and no other country wanted us, so we remained in Northern Rhodesia.

We knew nothing about my father until 1946, when my aunt in Poland wrote with the tragic news that he had been caught by the Soviets in 1944 and shot. His body was never recovered. I was 16 years old when we received this news, and I felt I had been robbed. My country, my baby sister, my cousin, and now my father had all been taken from me because of that horrible war. I had barely had a childhood.

I never returned to Poland. I no longer felt that it was my country. After my experiences, I could never live under Communism. Lwów, the town I so loved as a child, became part of Russia and then, after the fall of Communism, Ukraine.

In June 1947 I took a secretarial job with the Northern Rhodesian government. By the time the refugee

By 1946, when this photo was taken, my mother, Antek, and I were living in Africa in Northern Rhodesia. We were no longer the gaunt, starved figures that had sailed from Krasnovodsk.

camp closed in 1948, I had saved enough money to send Antek to boarding school in South Africa.

In 1954 I sailed to England for a six-month vacation. Ciocia Stefa and Wujcio Władzio now lived in London. There I met Franek, a Polish chemical engineering student at London University. Four months later we were engaged, but I had to return to my job in Africa.

Two months later Franek moved to Africa and got a job at a copper mine. On January 31, 1956, we were married. I moved from Ndola to Nkana, where he lived, and started working for the government medical bureau.

In June 1958 our son Andrew was born. By the time our daughter, Barbara, was born in January 1961, winds of change were blowing across Africa. Communists who had been trained in Russia and Cuba infiltrated the peaceful villages and towns. Violence against white people became common. In August 1962 we moved to Johannesburg, South Africa, where Antek was studying mining engineering. Our son Richard was born in December 1963.

But the political future of South Africa presented many problems. Riots erupted from time to time. We decided we didn't want to bring up our children under these conditions. When Antek received a scholarship to Stanford University in California in 1967, we decided to go to the United States. On June 29, 1969, we boarded the RMS *Windsor Castle* and sailed away from South Africa.

When we arrived on the US East Coast on July 29, Zosia, whom I had last seen in Persia in 1942, met us at the dock. She was now married with three children: Krysia, Renia, and Marek. Ciocia Stefa and Wujcio Władzio had been living with Zosia and her family in New Jersey since 1956. We stayed with them until Franek got a job in San Francisco. On October 19, 1969, we arrived in California and settled in the Bay Area. My journey across the world had finally ended.

A Guide to Geographical Names

The world has changed a great deal since my family and I were taken out of Poland in 1940. My own city of Lwów is now located in Ukraine, not Poland. Many of the small villages and settlements in Kazakhstan no longer exist. Many cities and countries throughout the world have new names. In this book, I have used the geographical names as they were when I traveled through, and lived in, these places. Here is a guide to the contemporary names of the places mentioned in this book, in alphabetical order by the original names.

THEN	NOW
Akdendek, Kazakhstan	No longer on the map
Alma Ata, Kazakhstan	Almaty

THEN	NOW
Czechoslovakia	Czech Republic and Slovakia
Georgiewka, Kazakhstan	Kalbatau, or Qalbatau
Krasnovodsk, Turkmenistan	Türkmenbaşy
Lwów, Poland	Lviv, Ukraine
Northern Rhodesia	Zambia
Semipalatynsk, Kazakhstan	Semey
Yangi Yul, Uzbekistan	Yangiyo'l, or Yangiyul

Acknowledgments

First of all, I would like to thank Elaine Starkman, my writing teacher at Diablo Valley College and California State University, East Bay. Without her encouragement, support, and belief in me, this book would not have been written. I would also like to thank all the students who participated in the writing classes with me for listening to my stories and offering their suggestions and support. I hold a special memory of one of the students, Dr. Roy Kahn, whose help I'm very grateful for. He passed away before this book was published, and will be greatly missed.

Great thanks go to my cousin and collaborator Krystyna Poray Goddu, who served as both editor and agent for this project, working with me for more than a decade to shape my stories into a book and then persevering to inspire an editor's interest. I'm very grateful to Lisa Reardon for being that editor—and for her excitement and enthusiastic belief that this story needed to be told. Many thanks to Lindsey Schauer and everybody at Chicago Review Press who helped make this book both look and read as beautifully as it does.

I am deeply grateful to my brother, Antek Mihulka, who lived through these years with me. He and I have spent a great deal of time discussing the many events that occurred, and his memory of so many details enriched my own.

Thank you to my children and grandchildren for their ongoing support of my writing. I'm especially grateful to my daughter, Barbara, who wanted me to write these stories down, and to my granddaughter Christina, who read them when she was a young girl and who urged me to keep writing. Christina also devoted her time and filmmaking skills to creating a promotional video for the book, which my cousin Krystyna and I appreciate very much. Thank you to my son Richard for his computer technology support in so many ways! I also want to thank my son Andrew for enlightening me regarding issues of historical perspective, which further motivated me to write this book.

Thanks to the authors and experts who helped with this book: Wesley Adamczyk, author of *When God Looked the Other Way*, for lending photography and sharing his expertise; Steven Barnes, professor of modern Russian and Soviet history at George Mason University and author of *The Wives' Gulag: The Akmolinsk Camp for Wives of Traitors to the Motherland*, for his insights into Kazakhstan geography; Vladimir Okhotin, representative of AboutKazakhstan.com, for additional geographical help; and Franek Rymaszewski, of www.rymaszewski.iinet.net.au, for lending photography.